FT. STODDART

FT. MONTGOMERY

MOBILE

TENSAS R.

NINET R.

O BILOXI

CEDAR R.

DARBONNE R.

PASCA GOULA R.

M O B I L E

B A Y

CRON PASS

GUILLORY

DAUPHINE I.

FT. BOWYER

EUR I.

BON SECOUR

BAY

FISH R.

STRUK R.

GEN. JACKSON'S MARCH TO PENSACOLA

CONNY R.

M

THE BARATARIANS
AND
THE BATTLE OF NEW ORLEANS

THE BARATARIANS

AND THE BATTLE OF

NEW ORLEANS

Jane Lucas de Grummond

LOUISIANA
STATE UNIVERSITY PRESS
BATON ROUGE

To

Ernest I, II and III

18852

Louisiana State University Press
Library of Congress Catalogue Card Number: 61-7540
Manufactured in the United States of America by
J. H. Furst Co., Baltimore 2, Maryland

Design by Ernst A. Seemann

TABLE OF CONTENTS

LIST OF ILLUSTRATIONS

INTRODUCTION

MOST ACCOUNTS OF THE BRITISH INVASION OF LOUISIANA describe fully the activities of Tennessee, Kentucky and Mississippi militia and give them the main credit for driving out the enemy. Baratarians and their associates, when mentioned, are disposed of briefly. They did not write the reports that were sent to Washington after the battle was over. From these records and published histories the reader does not realize that victory would have been impossible without the smugglers and privateers.

Jackson had used up all his ammunition and most of his flints during the Creek campaign. When he came to New Orleans at the beginning of December, 1814, he had a few troops, no artillery and no supplies. Yet from the night of December 23, 1814, to January 19 (not January 8), 1815, almost continuous bombardment harassed the British. Baratarians supplied the powder, flints, cannon, cannon balls, flying-angles, ship cannister, and " every description of destructive missile."

Cannon fire from the *Carolina* spearheaded the night attack of December 23. The battles on December 28 and January 1 were artillery duels. Riflemen from the Tennessee Valley were good shots on January 8 but after the first half hour they were not needed. The British retreated—and could not renew the battle because the artillery kept up its bombardment until the British asked for a truce several hours later. Reinforcements from England continued to arrive at the British camp, but eleven more days of bombardment killed any remnant of resistance that remained and caused the enemy to slink away.

Jackson's chief engineer, Major A. Lacarrière Latour, wrote the best account of the battle. This was published in 1816. In this work Latour could not do full justice to the Baratarians because he knew too much about them. He was a patriot during the battle, but he was not before; and soon afterwards he and the Laffites became spys and agents for Spain. In Spain's secret files, Pierre Laffite became No. 13-A or 13-*uno*; Jean Laffite became 13-B, 13 *dos* or 13 *bis*.; Latour travelled under the name of John Williams.

A review of Latour's book which appeared shortly after its publication shows the almost forgotten significance to the people of that generation of the War of 1812. In their eyes " all the disposable forces both sea and land, were directed to these devoted shores, which they (the British) were to overrun, and particular parts were to be retained as permanent acquisitions. An eminent Map-seller in London advised an American gentleman, not knowing him to be such, who applied to him for a map of the United States, to defer the purchase for a few weeks; that he was then keeping all his maps unfinished, as the boundaries would all be changed, and a considerable part of the Union incorporated with the British possessions! " [1]

The United States made many blunders during the war but the enemy committed still greater. When they found themselves unexpectedly relieved from the long contest in Europe, they should have offered peace. " This would have appeared the greatest magnanimity on their part, thus to waive the opportunity of overwhelming us. The capture of the frigates would have been forgotten and we should have escaped from a luckless war, with all the disgrace of our first defeats by land, and in the opinion of the world and perhaps our own, should have thought we owed our

---

[1] *The North American Review and Miscellaneous Journal*, III (July, 1816), 238.

escape to the clemency of a generous and powerful foe. . . . They came and were covered with confusion and disgrace." [2]

The author is deeply grateful for the patient help of the Louisiana State Library Staff, especially of the following: Vergil L. Bedsole, Virginia M. Ott and Marcelle F. Schertz, Archives; Elizabeth Welker, Government Documents; Lucy B. Foote, Evangeline M. Lynch and Emeline R. Staples, Louisiana Room; and George J. Guidry, Photo-duplications.

Raymond H. Downs, graduate student in history at Louisiana State University, found the roster of the Orleans Battalion in the Louisiana State Archives; he also found the letter in Appendix A.

In New Orleans the following were most helpful in locating documents: George Raffalovich, researcher; Connie G. Griffith, Tulane University Archives; Mary M. Impastato, Secretary, St. Louis Cathedral; Clarence Wagner, United States District Court; and Fordyce L. Perego.

Hazel Rodgers, Beth de Grummond, and Linda Johnson helped with the page proofs and Index.

Finally, mention must be made of Mildred and Darryl Smith with whom I explored Grande Terre; and of Lonie Vizier, " King of Cut Off," with whom I sailed out Barataria Pass in *Boston Bill*.

JANE LUCAS DE GRUMMOND

Baton Rouge, August 11, 1960.

---

[2] *Ibid.*, 237-38.

THE BARATARIANS
AND
THE BATTLE OF NEW ORLEANS

BARATARIA

AND THE BARATARIANS

THE FIRST SETTLERS IN LOUISIANA NEEDED TERMITE-RESISTANT cypress for building their houses and sturdy oaks for building their ships. Across the Mississippi from New Orleans was a lush forest of these timbers in a swamp area which was really an island because it was bounded by the Big Lake of the Ouatchas, the Ouatchas River, the Little Lake of the Ouatchas, and Bayou Pierrot.[1]

However, this swamp forest was inaccessible to those early Frenchmen, so they named it " The Island of Barataria," after that unattainable island kingdom of Sancho Panza in Cervantes' immortal *Don Quixote*.[2] In time the whole area west of New Orleans to Bayou Lafourche and south to the Gulf was called Barataria. One branch of the Ouatchas River snakes almost to the Mississippi where it curves below New Orleans; so the Ouatchas, " the bayou which leads to Barataria," came to be called Bayou Barataria. The bay into which this river, the two lakes, and numerous little bayous disembogue was called Barataria Bay.

This Bay is fifteen miles long and six wide. It is protected from the Gulf of Mexico by Grande Terre and Grand Isle, two islands that

---

[1] A. Lacarrière Latour, *Historical Memoir of the War in West Florida and Louisiana in 1814-1815* (Philadelphia, 1816), 13. On modern maps, Big Lake of the Ouatchas is Lake Salvador, and the other is Little Lake; Bayou Pierrot is Bayou Perot.

[2] Le Page du Pratz, *Histoire de la Louisiane* (3 vols., Paris, 1758), I, 289.

(3)

lie almost end to end. The pass between them that leads to the Gulf (Barataria Pass) is only a quarter of a mile wide. Grande Terre is the eastern island. It is about 40 miles due south of New Orleans and 70 miles west-northwest of the mouth of the Mississippi. Here the Laffite brothers established smuggling headquarters for privateers of the Gulf and the Caribbean who were driven from one French island after another.

This was during the period of the Napoleonic Wars when Creole corsairs harassed English shipping until Great Britain set to work in dead earnest to capture their bases. One of the first to fall was the island of Santa Lucia in 1803. During the course of the attack a Creole shot Edward Michael Pakenham in the neck. When this wound healed it drew his head to one side. Six years later Pakenham commanded at the capture of Martinique. Again he was shot in the neck. When this second wound healed it restored his head to its original position.[3]

Guadeloupe, the last of the French islands, fell to the English in February of 1810. After that date, privateers sailing under French commissions no longer had a harbor nor an admiralty court to which they could openly take their prizes. This did not stop them for they had already found Grande Terre. The first smugglers' convention had been held there in 1805. Among those present were Alexandre, Pierre and Jean Laffite, Vincent Gambie, Louis Chighizola and perhaps Renato Beluche also.[4] Jean Laffite emerged as the leader and organizing genius of the privateers.

The Laffite brothers were born at Port-au-Prince, Haiti. Their parents had moved there from Spain to escape the Inquisition which had persecuted and finally killed Mrs. Laffite's father. Alexandre Frederic, the oldest of eight children, was born in 1771. The youngest, Jean, was born in 1782. Pierre was two and a half years older than Jean. These two youngest brothers were inseparable in their play and studies. They did not remember their mother, who

---

[3] *Dictionary National Biography* (22 vols., London, 1949-50), XV, 83-84; Alexander Walker, *Jackson and New Orleans* (New York, 1856), 200-201.
[4] *The Journal of Jean Laffite* (New York, 1958), 38.

died soon after Jean was born, but their Jewish grandmother took her place and dominated their early lives. She planted a deep hatred of Spain in her grandsons; but she was an intelligent, educated woman and saw that they had competent tutors at home until Jean was fourteen. Then the two boys were sent to a private school on the island of Martinique. Later they had military training on another island, Saint Christopher; it was here that Jean became skilled in the use of duelling weapons.[5]

Meanwhile, Alexandre Frederic had become a privateer. Following the usual practice of those who followed this profession, he never revealed his true name or origin. To the enemies of France, upon whose commerce he preyed, he was known as Dominique You or Frederic You.

Dominique was short, not quite five feet four inches tall. His shoulders, twice as broad as the average man's, made him seem strong and stubborn as an ox. He was swarthy, with flashing black eyes and a hawk-like nose. Scars from powder burns on the left side of his face made him look ferocious, yet men soon discovered that he was a likable cuss.

Jean and Pierre were determined to become privateers like Dominique. While he was in France winning fame as a cannoneer, they trained in the Gulf and Caribbean under Renato Beluche who seemed mature to them because he already had twelve years' experience at sea. He was solidly built, with broad shoulders and a strong aquiline nose that showed he was kin to Dominque You. Although he was probably a second cousin of the Laffites and the same age as Pierre, Jean and Pierre called Renato " uncle."

Beluche was a native of New Orleans. He was born there in 1780.[6]

---

[5] *Journal of Jean Laffite*, 10; Stanley Clisby Arthur, *Jean Laffite, Gentleman Rover* (New Orleans, 1952), 283; Henry Adams, *History of the United States* (9 vols., New York, 1890 and 1930), VII, 321; Frank R. Stockton, *Buccaneers and Pirates on our Coasts* (New York, 1898), 281; Gaillard Hunt, *Life in America one hundred years ago* (New York, 1914), 162.

[6] St. Louis Cathedral Archives, New Orleans, Register I. Month and date of birth are not clear. The date appears to be December 15, 1780. Date of baptism is January 7, 1781. The Index to the Archives states the approximate year of the marriage of his

His birthplace was 632 Dumaine Street, the house known today as " Madam John's Legacy." [7]

Beluche was seven when his father died,[8] leaving a pregnant wife, five children, and, as far as property was concerned, one heavily mortgaged plantation and several slaves.[9] Selina, Renato's youngest sister, was born five months later.

Renato went to sea, shipping on fishing boats, smugglers, merchant vessels. He served his term on the governor's flagship and learned how to handle cannon.[10] Within a few years he was part-owner of at least two privateers and sailed under letters of marque from Guadeloupe. This island was the seat of French colonial government in the Lesser Antilles, therefore the source of privateer commissions and the haven to which prizes could be taken and lawfully condemned in admiralty court.

When the blacks in Haiti succeeded in driving out the French armies and establishing an independent republic, French Creoles fled to Louisiana. Jean and Pierre helped to transport many of these as well as their father, their youngest sister Yvonne and her family, and their own families.[11] Then the brothers returned to their privateering.

---

parents as 1767, and adds that the marriage record had been destroyed. His mother was Rosa Laporte of Orleans Parish; his father was Renato Beluche of Tours, France.

[7] George Cable made this house famous. It was the scene of his story about Tite Poulette, daughter of the beautiful quadroon Zalli and Monsieur John. When Monsieur John died, the house became known as " Madam John's Legacy," and that is the name by which it is known today, even though it is now part of the Louisiana State Museum.

Laura Porteous and Samuel Wilson searched the titles to this property. According to their findings, Santiago Lamelle sold the house to Renato Beluche Sr., in 1778; he in turn sold it in 1783 to Don Manuel de Lanzos. " Madam John's Legacy " is reputed to be the oldest house in the Mississippi Valley—built *circa* 1723. *Times Picayune, Sunday Magazine,* July 17, 1949, 13.

The last owner of the house was Mrs. I. I. Lemmann. She gave it to the Louisiana State Museum.

[8] The inscription on his tomb reads: " Renat Beluche, husband of Dona Rosa Laporte, Age 50 years, Died September 3, 1778." Saint Louis Cemetery No. 1, New Orleans.

[9] Cabildo Records, New Orleans, Document No. 2262, Box 55.

[10] Stanley Faye, " Privateers of Guadeloupe and Their Establishment in Barataria," *Louisiana Historical Quarterly,* XXIII (Baton Rouge, April, 1940), 429.

[11] Jean had married Christina Levine in the year 1800 at her home on the island of St. Croix. She was the daughter of Thomas Levine, a merchant through whom privateers

One day in June, 1805, Jean Laffite sailed up the Mississippi and anchored at the Crescent City. Dominique was there to greet him; he had recently returned from France. Anyone watching the two at that moment would never have guessed that the stocky, swarthy Dominique was conversing with his brother. Jean was five feet ten inches tall, but he seemed taller because he was slim and stood proudly erect. Some say he was fair with reddish blond hair and hazel eyes. Others say his hair was dark. Jean tells us that many times he washed his head with potash and gunpowder which made his hair, eyebrows, and mustache a beautiful red color.[12] Whatever the color of his hair, Jean was meticulous about his clothes and elegant in his manners. In fact, he was a handsome, refined gentleman.

Jean told Dominique that he had prize goods and 12,600 English pounds in hard money with him and that he needed an agent to help him dispose of these items in New Orleans. After making discreet inquiries, Jean went to Joseph Sauvinet, a shrewd Frenchman from Bayonne who had lived in New Orleans long enough to become one of its most important businessmen. He employed twenty clerks in his counting house in the suburb Marigny.[13]

Hard money was scarce in New Orleans. The main source of supply had been Mexico, but that had been cut off since 1803 when the United States purchased Louisiana. Spanish and French paper money was available, but citizens had little or no confidence in it. They resisted Governor William C. C. Claiborne's attempt to establish a bank. Such an institution was new to the Creoles. They thought it would issue paper money which to them would be the same as legalized robbery. Had they not already suffered greatly

---

did considerable business. Jean and Christina soon had two sons and, when they fled from Haiti in 1804, Christina died giving birth to a daughter. Jean named the baby Denise Jeannette. His sister Yvonne took the baby while Pierre's wife took the two boys. Pierre's wife was Françoise Sel, the daughter of Jean Baptiste l'Etang Sel, who had been a planter in Haiti. Sel became famous in New Orleans as a portrait and miniature painter. *Journal of Jean Laffite*, 21; Arthur, *Jean Laffite*, 19, 23, 255.

[12] *Journal of Jean Laffite*, 122.

[13] Vincent Nolte, *Fifty Years in Both Hemispheres* (New York, 1854), 207; Arthur, *Jean Laffite*, 20.

from the depreciation of French and Spanish paper? What better results could they expect from American paper?[14]

It was not much wonder that Sauvinet was impressed with Jean's 12,600 hard pounds. He became Jean's partner and told him that, in order to avoid greedy customs officials, he should in the future unload cargoes at a point, which he indicated on a map, down the river below English Turn; and that he, Sauvinet, would get them from that depot to his warehouses. This was the beginning of a contraband commercial venture that was to involve nearly everyone in New Orleans.

When Jean left the city, Dominique sailed with him. They had captured nearly a dozen English vessels by the time they found Pierre in Guadeloupe. Pierre was handsome and fair or dark like Jean, and the same height but he did not seem as tall. He was heavier and careless in appearance; and because he was not as " refined " as Jean, he had a great deal more pleasure with women.

Soon Renato Beluche arrived at Guadeloupe also. In between legitimate runs from New Orleans to Vera Cruz, Pensacola, or Havana,[15] Beluche found his way to the French islands with prizes he had captured. For his privateering ventures, he used a number of aliases—among them Pedro Brugman or variations thereof, and the name Rigmartin.[16]

As the English closed in on the French Islands, more and more contraband was taken to Grande Terre or other islands along the coast and smuggled up the bayous to Donaldsonville and New Orleans. In 1807, Jean acquired a warehouse in New Orleans. He built one the next year at Donaldsonville, and a relay warehouse at the village of Barataria.[17]

---

[14] Charles E. A. Gayarré, *History of Louisiana* (4 vols., New Orleans, 1903), IV, 15.

[15] Customs House Records show that on March 4, 1805, Beluche sailed the schooner *Two Sisters* to Vera Cruz for its owner, Bartholomew Bosque, listed as a New Orleans merchant, and in the fall another to Vera Cruz. Three voyages for other merchants and in other vessels are recorded for the year 1806, two for 1807, and one for 1808. Crew Lists, United States Customs Archives, Port of New Orleans, I (1803-1805), Book 2002, 16, 43, 52, 197; II (1806-1808), Book 2003, 83, 159, 212; Book 2005, 372, 449, 552.

[16] William B. Bollaert, " Life of Jean Laffite," *Littell's Living Age*, XXXII (Boston, March, 1852), 442.

[17] *Journal of Jean Laffite*, 39.

Late in that year, 1808, Jean passed the mouth of the Mississippi sailing west with four captured vessels in tow. One of these he had named the *Tigre*. It was to become Dominique's flagship.[18] The little fleet sailed through Barataria Pass, then turned east and anchored off the broad beach of Grande Terre. This island, six miles long and three wide, was flat, and when Jean first saw it only a few rude huts and scrub bushes broke its smooth contour. Now warehouses (within two years there would be forty of them), slave pens, dwellings, a hospital, and a fort were being built.

Soon a multitude of pirogues and other bayou craft converged at Grande Terre as news of Laffite's arrival spread through the labyrinth of Barataria. The contraband was unloaded on these small vessels. Then they sailed across Barataria Bay, through devious waterways to Little Lake, then up Barataria Bayou to its head across the Mississippi from New Orleans. It took three days for the pirogues to reach this spot. Men and mules were ready to transfer their contraband the short distance overland to the river where it was ferried across to the city. In this way the market was flooded with iron, wine, dry goods, and manufactured goods, as well as slaves. Prices dropped to amounts that people could afford to pay. Pig iron was one dollar per hundredweight. Ladies were happy and honest Anglo-Saxon merchants unhappy as the price of silk stockings dropped to nine dollars a dozen pairs.[19]

Chief among the other privateer captains who nosed along the Louisiana coast to Grande Terre were two Italians: Louis Chighizola and Vincent Gambie. Chighizola was a native of Genoa.[20] He had on his body scars of many a battle, but there was one on his face that made people stare and call him " Nez Coupé " (Cut Nose). A saber thrust had slashed off half his nose.

Vincent Gambie looked like the cruelest assassin alive, and legend and Spanish archives picture him as the blackest villain.[21] His

---

[18] United States District Court of Louisiana, Cases No. 812, No. 816.

[19] Faye, " Privateers of Guadeloupe," 442.

[20] USDC of La., Case No. 816.

[21] Stanley Faye, " Privateersmen of the Gulf and Their Prizes," *Louisiana Historical Quarterly,* XXII (Baton Rouge, October, 1939), 26-27 in the reprint. Faye cites

schooner he had named the *Philanthrope*, which was rather an odd name for a slaver; but perhaps Gambie felt that his black cargo would be better off in Louisiana and Mississippi than in Africa or Cuba.

The privateers were preying on Spanish commerce as well as English, for Spain was now openly allied with England in war against Napoleon. French refugees who had fled from Haiti to Cuba at the time that the Laffites had taken their families to New Orleans now found themselves persecuted. They escaped to Louisiana.

Perhaps it was because of his French Creole wife that Governor Claiborne was at first sympathetic to these French refugees—and did not molest the Baratarians who brought them. Claiborne reported in June, 1809, that "near one thousand people from Cuba have reached this City, and from two to three hundred more have passed the Balize.[22] Some of those arrived in great distress; . . . Their negro's are still detained on Board the Vessels in which they came— I should myself be well pleased if Congress would relax the Law forbidding the importation of Slaves,[23] as relates to these *miserable exiles*. I witness their distress, and would most readily alleviate it, if in my powers."[24]

An act was approved June 28, 1809, which authorized the President of the United States to remit penalties imposed under the exclusion act in cases where the owners of slaves had been expelled from

---

Papeles de Cuba, Legajo 1796, Soto to Apodaca, April 25, 1815, in which Gambie is described as "the cruelest and the greatest assassin among all the pirates."

[22] When the French first came to Louisiana, South East Pass was the only one of the five passes at the mouth of the Mississippi which could be used by vessels drawing fourteen feet of water. The French set up a pilot station at the head of this pass to guide ships seeking the mouth of the river. It became known as the Balize, from the French word for "beacon." Alcée Fortier, *Louisiana* (3 vols., Atlanta, 1909-14), I, 438.

[23] Act of March 2, 1807: "An Act to prohibit the importation of Slaves into any port or place within the jurisdiction of the United States, from and after the first day of January, in the year of our Lord one thousand eight hundred and eight." W. E. Burghardt Du Bois, *The Suppression of the African Slave-Trade to the United States of America 1683-1870* (New York, 1954), 94-108.

[24] Claiborne to Julien Poydras, June 4, 1809, in *The Territorial Papers of the United States*, ed. Clarence Edwin Carter (Washington, 1934—), IX, *The Territory of Orleans 1803-1812* (1940).

Cuba.[25] So slave-owning refugees, and refugees who were free people of color, and free Negroes continued to swell the population of New Orleans.

By July of 1809, the record shows that 5,754 emigrants had come to New Orleans. Of this number 1,798 were white French; 1,977 were free colored and free black; and 1,979 were slaves.[26] By the end of the year the population of New Orleans had doubled and more than half this number were recent French arrivals.[27] The Anglo-Saxon and Spanish elements found themselves very much in the minority, and they resented and feared the French Creoles as their influence dominated not only in the city, but in the whole delta area.

One has only to look at Crew Lists in the Customs House Records to discover where the free colored and free blacks found employment. The 30 or more privateer captains who sailed out of Barataria had small vessels, 120- or 130-ton brigs and schooners, but they manned them with crews of 90 to 170 and sometimes even 200 men. These men were trained as cannoneers as well as deck hands. On a successful cruise a captain might take six or more prizes. Some of these would be sunk or otherwise destroyed after the removal of cargo, but good vessels were saved and had to be manned by prize crews.

A conservative estimate of the number of Baratarians who served on the fleet would be 3,000 men.[28] A similar number must have served on shore to unload goods and get them to distributing centers, to corral captured slaves until they were sold, and to transport powder and flint to ammunition depots in the interior. Some writers estimate that Jean and Pierre Laffite controlled an organization of more than 5,000 men. This is probably an understatement.

[25] *Ibid.*, 843.

[26] Gayarré, *History of Louisiana*, IV, 218.

[27] Dunbar Rowland (ed.), *Official Letter Books of W. C. C. Claiborne, 1801-1816* (6 vols., Jackson, 1907), IV, 358-67, 372, 378; Faye, " Privateers of Guadeloupe," 435; William O. Scroggs, *The Story of Louisiana* (Indianapolis, 1924), 204-205.

[28] These figures, as well as the size of vessels and crews, are based on piracy case records in USDC of La. and on Customs House Records.

Commodore Patterson found about 1,000 on Grande Terre alone during his raid in September, 1814.

A new source of privateer commissions and a new port opened to the Baratarians at the close of 1811—Spain's most strongly fortified city in the new world, Cartagena, on the Caribbean coast of South America. This seaport was the capital of Cartagena province, a part of New Granada (today the state of Colombia). Cartagena declared its independence from Spain on November 11, 1811. Immediately Spanish troops cut off her source of supplies from the interior. The President of Cartagena retaliated by sending a vessel with privateer commissions to Grande Terre and by inviting the Baratarians to capture or destroy Spanish shipping.[29] The Baratarians were quick to accept the commissions which they needed to supplement their French ones; but because the United States was not at war with Spain, they still could not legally bring into the United States any prizes they might capture.

This did not alter the operations of Baratarians. They continued to infest all approaches to Cuba, since that island was the center of the slave trade. Soon the Spanish Consul at New Orleans was bombarding Governor Claiborne with complaints of illegal seizures.

Claiborne's young French wife had died after two brief years of marriage and he was now courting Sophronie Bosque, a Spanish señorita.[30] He was beginning to turn against the Baratarians, but the first to take definite action against them was Commodore David Porter of the United States Navy. No special machinery had been provided to enforce the act of March 2, 1807, which prohibited importation of slaves; and at first this duty fell to the Secretary of the Treasury as head of customs collections. Then, through the activity of cruisers, the Secretary of Navy came to have oversight of violations.[31]

Naval officials were stationed at the Balize to prevent the entry

---

[29] José Manuel Restrepo, *Historia de la Revolución de la República de Colombia* (4 vols., Besanzon, 1858), I, 155; USDC of La., Cases No. 746, No. 779, No. 817.

[30] Henry E. Chambers, *A History of Louisiana* (3 vols., Chicago, 1925), III, 370; Fortier, *Louisiana*, I, 214.

[31] Du Bois, *Suppression of Slave-Trade*, 108.

of suspected slavers or contraband, but there was not much they could do at this time because the Baratarians operated through the whole coastal area west of Grande Terre and Grand Isle. Chenière Caminada, the mouth of Bayou Lafourche, Timbalier Island, Cat Island and Isle Dernière all offered easy access to the Baratarian country. So great was the contraband they brought in that every month Laffite built a new warehouse in the area between Grande Terre and New Orleans, and now not only Sauvinet but a whole flock of merchants were his distributors.

Commodore Porter was indignant at the flagrant flouting of the laws of the United States. He reported that "the district attorney apparently winked at piracies committed in our waters and at the open communication kept up between these depredators and the citizens of New Orleans." [32]

Porter was aware of the complaints of the Spanish Consul and of the fact that Cuban merchants had subscribed $60,000 as a reward for three vessels which the privateers had taken.[33] These three vessels (the *Duc de Montebello*, *L'Epine*, and *Intrépide*) arrived at the Balize in the spring of 1810 and asked for "refreshment and repairs."

From the records it is difficult to say who was commanding these vessels. Testimony in piracy cases indicates time and again that captains frequently changed their names and the names of their vessels. Francis Brosquet may have been commanding the *Duc de Montebello*. Ange-Michel Brouard, alias Mentor, and perhaps alias Renato Beluche, was mentioned as the owner.[34] The *Duc de Montebello* brought a sheaf of French commissions. One of these was for Pedro Brugman, which name Beluche most frequently used as an alias.

Beluche was on the *Intrépide* which was listed as Sauvinet's vessel. Marcellin Batigne was serving at this time as master of *L'Epine*.

---

[32] David D. Porter, *Memoir of Commodore David Porter of the United States Navy* (Albany, 1875), 79.

[33] *Ibid.*, 81.

[34] Rowland (ed.), *Claiborne Letter Books*, V, 26; USDC of La., Case No. 363.

As soon as naval officials on duty at the Balize reported the arrival of these vessels to Porter in New Orleans, he went down the river with a force of gun boats and demanded that the privateers surrender. They refused and the District Attorney asked Porter to let the vessels depart. " The many friends of the buccaneers in New Orleans made every exertion to obtain permission for them to depart," reported Porter, " and a direct conflict arose between the civil and naval authority, which culminated when Commander Porter informed the privateer captains that in default of their immediate surrender he should open fire." [35]

The privateers hauled down their colors, and Porter took the three vessels to New Orleans and began proceedings to claim them as prizes in the United States District Court. It was now the duty of the District Attorney to prosecute. Porter began to experience all of the ramifications and procrastinations of expert legal guidance in the courts. His lawyer Edward Livingston, whose wife was from Haiti and whose brother-in-law was from Haiti, must have laughed inwardly at his client's frustrations.

Porter recorded that all three prizes were condemned and sold, but apparently Sauvinet's *Intrépide* went free after paying a $1500 penalty; and when Customs refused her a clearance, she sailed without one.[36] *L'Epine*, " whose complete innocence had been proved," went out with the *Intrépide*.[37]

Porter's share in the prize money was one-fourth or $25,000. He had to pay Edward Livingston 5 per cent of this.[38] Then Porter, with proof of his capture of the three vessels, went to Havana to collect the $60,000 reward that the merchants had offered. He was " kept so long dancing attendance that he was very nearly impoverished." The promised reward was never paid.[39]

By mid-August the *Intrépide* was approaching Barataria with a

---

[35] Porter, *Memoir*, 79.
[36] Faye, " Privateers of Guadeloupe," 437, quoting from *Archivo General de Indias, Papeles de Cuba, Legajo* 1710, Morphy to Someruelos, May 30, 1810; USDC of La., Case No. 379.
[37] *Ibid.*
[38] Faye, " Privateers of Guadeloupe," 437; Porter, *Memoir*, 80-81.
[39] Porter, *Memoir*, 81.

prize when a storm blew the two vessels on the coast. Their cargoes of iron, wine and dry goods were unloaded on small craft and sent up the bayous while the wrecks were burned.[40]

Soon *L'Epine* neared the Mississippi with a prize, the *Alerta*, which had a cargo of slaves. Naval officials seized the *Alerta* and presented claim to its cargo in the United States District Court.[41] The slaves were ordered appraised and sold in accordance with an act passed by the legislature of the Territory of Orleans on March 16, 1810. This act said that slaves imported in violation of the act of March 2, 1807, " should be sold in the manner directed by the said act and that the proceeds of such sale should be delivered into the hands of the Marshal of said Territory, to be afterwards disposed of as the Legislature should deem proper." [42]

The slaves were quartered on Dr. William Flood's plantation on the west bank of the Mississippi and there appraised as follows: [43]

60 men at $400	$24,000
33 females at $325	10,725
51 boys and men, average $200	10,200
1 boy very sick	50
	$44,975

The value of this contraband is significant when one considers that for every prize libelled in court, dozens successfully unloaded at Barataria.

---

[40] *Louisiana Gazette*, July 28, August 23, September 4, 1810.
[41] USDC of La., Cases No. 379, No. 380, No. 381, No. 401.
[42] The act of March 16, 1810, is cited in Case No. 401.
[43] USDC of La., Case No. 380.

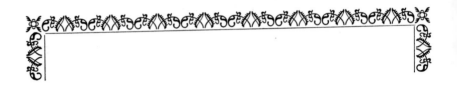

BARATARIA'S HEYDAY

Sugar planters, cotton planters, and merchants of all the lower part of the Mississippi Valley went to Grande Terre to buy slaves and British manufactured goods.[1] But Grande Terre was a three-days' journey from New Orleans. It was early in 1812 that Jean Laffite decided to hold an auction at The Temple.

The Temple was a chenière or mound of shells which Indians had built long before white men came to Louisiana. The mound covered a large area and was three or four feet higher than the surrounding marsh land which meant that it was dry. The Temple was located about half way between New Orleans and Grande Terre at the point where Bayou Pierrot and Bayou Barataria empty into Little Lake.

The auction was a huge success. Many more followed and so great was the demand for Baratarian wares that traders gave and received orders for them on the streets of New Orleans with as little secrecy as orders were given for purchases in Philadelphia or New York.[2]

Beluche, Dominique, Pierre Laffite, Gambie, and others paraded the streets of New Orleans arm in arm—singing, carousing in happy-

---

[1] Nolte, *Fifty Years in Both Hemispheres*, 189; Latour, *Historical Memoir*, 15.
[2] Latour, *Historical Memoir*, 15.

go-lucky fashion. Jean Laffite walked the streets openly but he found entertainment in more select circles. There seemed to be no limit to the success of the Baratarians; but, as in a Greek tragedy, their very success (which seemed like arrogance and insolence to certain Anglo-Saxon merchants who did not patronize them) provoked not " the wrath of heaven," but slow, inexorable Nemesis on the part of federal authorities and Governor Claiborne.

That section of the Louisiana Purchase which had been designated as the Territory of Orleans in 1804, became the State of Louisiana in 1812, and the legislature elected Claiborne as the first state governor. Six weeks after Louisiana became a state, the United States Congress declared war on Great Britain. On that same day, June 18, Congress authorized the President to issue commissions or letters of marque and general reprisal to private armed vessels, in such form as he should think proper and under the seal of the United States, against the vessels, goods, and effects of the government of the United Kingdom of Great Britain and Ireland, their dependencies, and the subjects thereof.[3] Six privateers were duly commissioned in New Orleans. Beluche accepted command of one of them, the four-gun schooner *Spy*, and he was the only one of the six who was successful.[4]

On the 17th of November, Beluche captured the 332-ton *Jane* laden with mahogany and logwood from Honduras. He took his prize to New Orleans and presented his claims in Admiralty Court.

The captain of the *Jane* declared before Judge Dominick Augustin Hall that the pretense upon which the ship was taken was her being British property, that resistance was made at the time of her capture, " that there were twelve carried guns mounted on board said vessel; that there were a few small arms on board, three kegs of powder and different kinds of shot; that she was so armed for the purpose of resisting any cruiser that might attack her." [5]

---

[3] USDC of La., Case No. 552.
[4] Edgar Stanton Maclay, *A History of American Privateers* (New York, 1899), 322.
[5] USDC of La., Case No. 552.

(17)

This suit speedily came to an end and Judge Hall decreed that "the said ship *Jane*, her tackle, apparel and furniture, guns and cargo, were rightly and duly taken and seized as aforesaid, and did at the time of the capture and seizure thereof, as far as appears to me, belong to Great Britain, or to some person or persons being subjects of the King of Great Britain . . . and as such ought to be accounted and reputed liable to confiscation and be adjudged as good and lawful prize to the said private armed schooner *Spy*, and the said ship *Jane*, her tackle, apparel and furniture, guns and cargo, be adjudged and condemned as good and lawful prize to the said Reyne Beluche, commander of the said private armed schooner *Spy*." [6]

The ease and quickness with which this case was settled and the fact that Beluche was awarded the captured ship and cargo which he had openly and legally brought into New Orleans should have made privateering for the United States attractive to the Baratarians. But *only six* privateers were commissioned by the federal government in New Orleans. British warships were patrolling the coast and beginning that tight blockade which would cause cotton and sugar of the Mississippi delta to pile up in warehouses for the next two and a half years.

Baratarians found Spanish prizes more numerous and more rewarding than British merchantmen. So the Spanish Consul had plenty of complaints which he filed with Claiborne while the federal government complained of the small customs receipts and the continued illegal importation of slaves, and Anglo-Saxon merchants insisted that something must be done.

So Andrew Hunter Holmes of the United States Army was sent "with a party of between 30 and 40 men . . . for the purpose of aiding revenue officers in preventing the practice of smuggling by means of Lake Barataria." Holmes and his men had proceeded as far as twenty-five miles into the Barataria country without witnessing any violation of the revenue law, when on the night of November 15, 1812, they hailed a pirogue. On its refusing to come on shore

---

[6] *Ibid.*; *Minutes United States District Court 1811-1815* (Typescript, Louisiana State University Library), III, 154.

Holmes " fired his piece without injurious effects " and the pirogue came to shore. It was found to have on board a small quantity of imported goods which Holmes took out and then " permitted the men to proceed in consequence of their behavoiring well after the capture." [7]

The next night, in the bright moonlight, Holmes and his men saw three or four sail upon the lake " which is the first large one after leaving the Temple." The federal men immediately got in boats and pursued the Baratarians. When they were within hailing distance, the Baratarians asked, " What boat is that? "

Holmes replied, " United States troops! "

Then in broken English a voice warned the troops that if they came nearer the Baratarians would fire into them and kill everyone. Holmes paid no attention to this threat and after a brief battle the Baratarians surrendered. Later a boat tried to escape, but some of the troops fired into it, killed one man and took the rest prisoners. Then all the prisoners and boats were rowed across the lake to Holmes's camp.

One of the boats was found to contain imported goods " consisting of a large quantity of cinnamon and other articles." Then Holmes brought " the whole of the goods and boats and all the prisoners except one who escaped a few miles above the city," to New Orleans.

The names of the prisoners, " as they confessed themselves were: Jean Laffite (jeune), Angel Raballo, Antoine Sennet, Antoine Angelet, Antoine Bormet, Pierre Cadet, Pierre Laffite (ainé), Jean Gentil, Salvador Artugue, Louis Dalhier, Jean Baptiste Soulize, Pierre Terraim, Michel Joseph, Andre Como, Henry Nuñez, Henry Seybardier, Antoine Michel, Manuel Garcia, Jean Herven, Julien Berat, Jean Mayer, Manuel Brazo, Martin Pounce, Antoine Cordier." [8]

This list is significant. It contains not a single Anglo-Saxon name. Most of the names are French, probably aliases, but the names of men from Haiti. Jean, the younger Laffite, and Pierre, the elder,

[7] USDC of La., Case No. 573.
[8] *Ibid.*

immediately secured bail. They had the best legal counsel in New Orleans—Edward Livingston.

The capture of the Baratarians was made on November 12, 1812. District Attorney John Randolph Grymes did not file a petition against them until April 7, 1813; that is, after Governor Claiborne had complained to the President and in the press, and had issued a proclamation on March 15, 1813, commanding the Baratarians to cease from their unlawful acts.[9]

Then Grymes most respectfully showed that Jean Laffite of the city of New Orleans was indebted to the United States for the sum of $12,014.52 for 26 bales cinnamon, 54 linen shirts, 3 pieces of Russia sheeting, 7 pieces canvas, 1 bundle twine, 1 piece of handkerchiefs—to the value of $4,004.89; these " being goods, wares and merchandise arriving from a foreign port or place within four leagues of the coast of the said United States and unladed from out of the said ship or vessel before said ship or vessel had arrived at the proper place for the discharge of her cargo or any part thereof and without the authorization of the proper officer or officers of the customs. . . . By virtue of the act of Congress of the United States . . . the said Jean Laffite hath forfeited and become liable to pay to the said United States treble the value of said goods." [10]

United States Marshal Pierre Le Breton Duplessis was given a writ on April 8, which commanded him " to take the body of Jean Laffite, so that he shall appear before this District Court on the third Monday of April." He was given a similar writ for Pierre. On April 19, Duplessis wrote on the writs, " Not to be found." He was given writs a second time on April 29, on which he wrote on July 20, " Not to be found." July 29, he was given a third set of writs. These he kept until October 16, then wrote on them, " Not to be found." [11]

Three times court had convened and Jean and Pierre had not appeared because Marshal Duplessis could not find them. Governor

---

[9] Gayarré, *History of Louisiana*, IV, 289-91; Arthur, *Jean Laffite*, 28.
[10] USDC of La., Case No. 573.
[11] *Ibid.*

Claiborne issued a second proclamation denouncing the Baratarians as bandits and ordering them to break up their establishment. Then throughout the city, he had the following notice posted:

I, governor of the state of Louisiana, offer a reward of five *hundred* Dollars which will be paid out of the Treasury, to any person delivering John Laffite to the Sheriff of the Parish of Orleans, or to any other Sheriff in the State, so that he, the said John Laffite, may be brought to justice.

> Given under my hand at New Orleans on the
> 24th day of November, 1813.
>
> William C. C. Claiborne.[12]

Two days later citizens guffawed as another handbill appeared in public places. It read something like this:

I, Bos of Barataria, offer a reward of five thousand dollars which will be paid out of my treasury, to any person delivering Governor Claiborne to me at Isle au Chat (Cat Island) west of Grande Terre, near the mouth of Bayou Lafourche.

> Given under my hand at Grande Terre on the
> 26th day of November, 1813.
>
> Jean Laffite.[13]

---

[12] Gayarré, *History of Louisiana*, IV, 302-303; Arthur, *Jean Laffite*, 31, cites the entire proclamation Claiborne issued that day against the Baratarians—what appeared on the handbill was the last part of that proclamation; Rowland, *Letter Books of Claiborne*, VI, 279-280.

[13] Letter of Walker Gilbert to Thomas Freeman. Donaldson Ville, February 18, 1814 (written about three months after the incident), Records of the Eastern District, State Land Office of Louisiana (see Appendix A); Letter of Major General Flournoy who succeeded General James Wilkinson as commander of the 7th military district to J. F. H. Claiborne, undated, J. F. H. Claiborne, *Life and Times of Gen. Sam Dale The Mississippi Partisan* (New York, 1860), 87-89. In part this letter says:

. . . A man called Laffite, reputed to be connected with smugglers and pirates, I determined to apprehend. I had a consultation with the governor, and we fixed a plan. I learned that he kept a mistress on Conti Street, and that he was expected to visit her on a certain night. I sent a corporal and six men to arrest him, but failed. The next day I ascertained that Laffite was in the house and in bed at the time, but, on hearing the approach of my guard, had leaped out of a window and into a well close by, where he remained, with his head only out of water, until the guard retired. I likewise received a message about him, stating that he knew me well; that he crossed me on my walks every night, and could slay me, or have me slain, at any moment, either in the streets or in my quarters; but that, as he knew I was acting from a sense of duty, he would spare me if I would take no farther cognizance of him. Having failed in my plan, Governor Claiborne said he would see what he

Meanwhile, the British tried several times in that year of 1813, to invade Barataria; but the privateers were better gunners and the British retired suffering losses. In August, Dominique, Gambie and Jean Marotte attacked an English convoy in the neighborhood of Barbados. After a hot battle they succeeded in detaching two slavers which they captured and brought to Grande Terre. Then the British tried different tactics. Just a few days before Claiborne published his proclamation offering a $500 reward for Jean Laffite, a British man-of-war appeared at Grande Terre and one of its officers tried to get permission for the British to fortify channels so that they could pass secretly through Barataria to New Orleans. Jean told the officer that warships of the United States were nearby at Timbalier Island. The man-of-war hastily sailed away.[14]

In early April, 1814, Dominique sailed from Grande Terre in the *Tigre* searching for prey. He spied sail to the west and followed for a day when he discovered he was chasing a British armed merchantman. On the Mexican coast north of Vera Cruz, off the port of Nautla, the *Tigre* attacked the merchantman. Dominique's cannon were deadly and the battle was soon over. Delirious with joy, the jubilant buccaneers celebrated.

" Whiskey! For all hands! " roared Dominique.

Suddenly the roistering crew was knocked sprawling to the deck. The *Tigre* had wrecked on a shoal. Shocked sober, the sailors looked lugubriously at one another.

" Don't look like that," pleaded Dominique. " Sapristi! I can get another ship. There are plenty more where this one came from."

High spirits returned as the Baratarians scrambled to shore. Some men from Nautla had been watching them and asked who they were. " Baratarians," was the reply.

---

could do in the matter; that Laffite had comrades who would betray him. He offered a reward of five hundred dollars for his apprehension. Next, day, a proclamation, signed Laffite, appeared, offering *five thousand dollars* for the governor's head! He added a postscript, however, stating that this was a mere *bagatelle*. He was subsequently pardoned by the governor, and assisted in the defense of New Orleans. I know not what became of him thereafter.

(The author is indebted to Fordyce L. Perego of New Orleans for this citation.)

[14] *Journal of Jean Laffite*, 50-51.

The men from Nautla knew about Grande Terre. They were Mexican patriots and had captured a Spanish felucca which they wanted Dominique to take and bring back loaded with arms and ammunition. General Juan Pablo Anaya was to accompany them and pay them $10,000 in silver.[15]

Dominique jumped at the chance to make such a deal. Hard money was still scarce in New Orleans. He knew that merchants, bankers, and others would be only too glad to take part in such commerce.

And so it was at this time that the New Orleans Association took definite shape. Edward Livingston was the directing genius of the group which included John Randolph Grymes, district attorney; Abner L. Duncan, former territorial attorney general at Natchez; John K. West, Duncan's business partner; United States Marshal Pierre Le Breton Duplessis; Benjamin Morgan, bank president; Captain Henry Perry, quartermaster and ordnance officer in New Orleans, and a number of others.[16] This group of men saw that Laffite's magazines were filled with powder and flints.

So Dominique was able to load the felucca with 80,000 pounds of gunpowder and return to Nautla by June 20. This was the beginning of a flourishing trade between the New Orleans Association and the Mexican patriots.[17]

While Dominique was busy along the Gulf coast, Beluche was at Cartagena, transporting troops for the new republic and helping rescue survivors of an expedition against the Spaniards at Santa Marta. For this service he was rewarded with the rank of *teniente de navío* in the Cartagenan navy.[18] Then he raided Spanish shipping.

At this time he had two vessels: *La Popa*, his favorite which he

---

[15] Faye, "Privateersmen of the Gulf and Their Prizes," 22; USDC of La., Case No. 817.

[16] Stanley Faye, "Commodore Aury," *Louisiana Historical Quarterly*, XXIV (Baton Rouge, July, 1941), 21 in the reprint.

[17] Faye, "Privateersmen of the Gulf," 22; USDC of La., Case No. 817.

[18] Hoja de Servicio, Archivo Nacional, Bogotá; Restrepo, *Historia de Colombia*, I, 177-78, 198-204; Renato Beluche, *R. Beluche, Capitán de navío de la República de Colombia* (Caracas, 1824; reprinted by Isidro Beluche in Panama, 1954), 4 in the original.

usually commanded himself and which had a crew of a hundred men; and the *Piñeres*, commanded by Charles Lominé. Beluche soon had a third ship. On October 2, 1813, he captured the 1012-ton *La Caridad*, alias *La Cubana*, as she was coming from New Haven to Cuba. Beluche changed her name to *Atalanta*, and later changed it again to *General Bolivar*.[19] This vessel was commanded by different captains or perhaps by the same captain under different names.

Beluche's service record says that during the three years he sailed under the flag of Cartagena he destroyed more than a million dollars worth of Spanish shipping. He prowled in the Bahama Channel, the Gulf, and the Caribbean, and kept Grande Terre supplied with commissions from Cartagena.

Gambie, with a fresh Cartagenan commission, was cruising along the Mexican coast in May, 1814. His good *Philanthrope* had a prize in tow, the schooner *Marcela*. Then off the bar of Tampico he captured another, the Spanish brig *Fernando VII*, Captain Vincente Quintanilla, of Campeche.

Back at Grande Terre the two prizes yielded their rich cargo. A few days later the Spanish Consul in New Orleans found a note on his desk written by Captain Quintanilla. It said: " Captain Gambie brought us to Grande Terre where he sold the cargo of my ship and that of the schooner *Marcela*. After keeping us twenty-eight days in the most cruel situation, this man had the kindness to give us the schooner *Marcela* in order that we may go to Campeche, our home port.[20]

Gambie usually was not so considerate. In fact, he had little respect for Jean Laffite's regulations against piracy. On one occasion the two clashed after Gambie attacked a merchantman of the United States.[21] Laffite won this battle of wills and in a few days Gambie seemed to have forgotten the incident as other events demanded attention.

---

[19] USDC of La., Cases No. 746, No. 760.
[20] Faye, " Privateersmen of the Gulf," 26-27, citing *AGI, PdeC, Legajo* 1836, Quintanilla to Morphy, June 29, 1814.
[21] Saxon, *Laffite the Pirate*, 49-51.

NEGRIL BAY

THE WAR OF 1812 WAS IN ITS THIRD YEAR BEFORE LOUISIANA became the theater of operations, but citizens there had been following developments with interest. They knew that peace overtures had been made almost as soon as the war began. However, it was not until the fall of 1813 that England agreed to meet American commissioners at some neutral city in Europe.

American commissioners arrived at Ghent in Belgium in the spring of the next year and cooled their heels waiting for their opponents. " England was gathering her strength to bludgeon America into submission and the British Cabinet was organizing as great an effort as they believed the British taxpayers would endure." [1] It was summer before the English commissioners arrived and with demands that took away the breath of the Americans.

They demanded a new boundary line between Canada and the United States which placed part of Maine, Vermont, and New York in Canada. From there the proposed line ran from the St. Lawrence to the Lakes, through Lake Erie to the head of the Allegheny River, down that river to the Ohio, from the Ohio to the Mississippi, and up the Mississippi to the Missouri, and following that river to the Rocky Mountains. The United States was to cede New Orleans,

---

[1] C. S. Forester, *The Age of Fighting Sail* (New York, 1956), 202.

" in order to insure us the enjoyment of our privileges to navigate the Mississippi." [2] These demands indicated that England still refused to recognize the Louisiana Purchase as legitimate.

So unthinkable were the British terms that the five Americans rejected them without even referring them to their government. The English commissioners stalled, waiting to hear that Great Britain was in possession of the Atlantic seaboard, Louisiana, and the whole Mississippi Valley. The course of war in Europe as well as in America gave them every reason to hope for such a result. Napoleon had been defeated. Britain's military might and all the resources of her Empire could now be used for a last stupendous effort to crush the United States.

The British press set to work to marshal opinion against the United States as it had against Napoleon. The London *Courier*, usually the first to receive information from the British ministry, reported January 27, 1814, on President Madison's annual message to Congress, saying that it was " a compound of canting and hypocracy, of exaggeration and falsehood, of coarseness without strength, of assertions without proof, of the meanest prejudices, and of the most malignant passions; of undisguised hatred of Great Britain, and of ill-concealed partiality and servility toward France."

The London *Times* on May 24, called Madison a liar and an imposter. It said, " Mr. Madison's dirty, swindling manoeuvres in respect to Louisiana and the Floridas remain to be punished. . . . With Madison and his perjured set no treaty can be made, for no oath can bind them." When British commissioners were ready to start for Ghent in June, the *Times* on the second of that month instructed them saying: " Our demands may be couched in a single word,—Submission."

On September 3, after the capture and burning of Washington (August, 1814), the *Sun* spoke of Americans as " worthless, lying, treacherous, false, slanderous, cowardly. . . . Were it not that the

---

[2] A London pamphlet entitled " compendious view of the points to be discussed in treating with the United States . . ." quoted in *Niles' Register* (76 vols., Baltimore, 1811-49), VII (December 10, 1814), 218.

course of punishment they are undergoing is necessary to the ends of moral and political justice, we declare before our country that we should feel ashamed of victory over such ignoble foes. The quarrel resembles one between a gentleman and a chimney-sweeper; the former may beat the low scoundrel to his heart's contentment; but there is no honor in the exploit, and he is sure to be covered with the soil and dirt of his ignominious antagonist."

As this hate campaign continued, the English were so sure of conquering the United States that the day after the news of the burning of Washington reached Europe, Paris newspapers reported Lord Castlereagh as saying: " I expect at this time most of the largest seaport towns in America are laid in ashes, that we are in possession of New Orleans, and have command of all the waters of the Mississippi and the lakes, so that now the Americans are little better than prisoners at large in their own country." [3]

Because of a change in naval command in 1814, the British offensive against the Atlantic coast was much more aggressive and effective than it had previously been. At the beginning of April Vice-Admiral Sir Alexander Cochrane arrived in Bermuda to supercede Admiral John Warren in command of the North Atlantic, Leeward Islands, and Jamaica stations.

Admiral Cochrane dispatched the *Orpheus*, Captain Pigot, to Apalachicola to negotiate with the Creeks and other Indians. The *Orpheus* arrived at Apalachicola May 10th, and within ten days Pigot estimated that 2,800 Creek warriors, perhaps as many Choctaws, and 1,000 others were ready to take up arms with the British. They would be easy to train because they were good horsemen and familiar with firearms. Pigot felt also that the Negroes of Georgia would join the British wholesale, once the movement started.

He suggested to Cochrane that, since Mobile was the only post held by the United States between Pensacola and Baton Rouge, a few British troops cooperating with Creeks and Choctaws could get possession of Baton Rouge. This would cut off New Orleans from

---

[3] *Niles' Register*, VII (February 18, 1815), 389.

the interior and make it easier to occupy that city and the lower Mississippi area.[4]

Cochrane felt that Pigot was right, so he reported to the Admiralty that not more than 3,000 British troops would be needed to drive Americans out of Louisiana and the Floridas. The 3,000 British troops could be landed at Mobile where Indians and disaffected French and Spaniards would join them.[5]

Meanwhile, Cochrane sent Colonel Edward Nicholls to Pensacola with 4 officers, 11 noncommisioned officers and 97 privates of the Royal Marines to train the Indians. They were dispatched in the *Hermes* and *Carron*. These sloops carried two howitzers, a field-piece, 1,000 stand of arms and 300 suits of clothing for the Indians. At the same time the brig *Orpheus* anchored at Apalachicola with 22,000 stand of arms, ammunition, blankets and clothing.[6]

While Nicholls was preparing the Florida thrust toward Louisiana, and while 10,000 veteran troops in Canada were ready to invade New York from Montreal by way of Plattsburgh and Lake Champlain, Cochrane terrorized the Atlantic coast to divert attention and military support from the two main targets of the British. His forces started on the coast of Maine, raided, ruthlessly looted, and worked their way south.

In August Cochrane's forces were augmented by the arrival of Admiral Malcolm and his fleet with additional regiments from Europe. It was not at all unusual for women to accompany such expeditions and there were women with this one. Balls and other public entertainments had been held through the fleet while crossing the Atlantic.

One night a grand ball was held on the Admiral's flag ship, the *Royal Oak*. It was opened " by Admiral Malcolm and the Honour-

---

[4] A. T. Mahan, *Sea Power in its Relations to the War of 1812* (2 vols., Boston, 1905), II, 383.

[5] *Ibid.*, 384.

[6] Latour, *Historical Memoir*, 10-11; Adams, *History of the United States*, VIII, 319-20; George Laval Chesterton, *Peace, War and Adventure* (2 vols., London, 1853), I, 213; Benson Earle Hill, *Recollections of an Artillery Officer* (2 vols., London, 1836), I, 299.

able Mrs. Mullens, in a country dance."[7] It is well to note the popularity of Mrs. Mullens with superior officers because it may have had some bearing on the truculence of her husband, Colonel Mullens, later at the battle of New Orleans.

After burning Washington and attacking Baltimore, Admiral Cochrane and his fellow officers agreed in conference that they had fulfilled their mission—harrying the Atlantic coast. Now it was time to withdraw from this diversionary movement and concentrate forces for the invasion of Louisiana.

On the west coast of Jamaica are two headlands eight miles apart, which protect an expanse of sea where ships can ride safely at anchor. This roadstead is called Negril Bay. Here British naval and military forces concentrated in November of 1814. Orders for this operation were written *after* peace commissioners had assembled at Ghent.

An English subaltern recorded that after the fleets had reached Negril Bay, "seventy or eighty sail of vessels . . . lay . . . so closely wedged together that to walk across the decks, from one to the other, seemed, when at a little distance, to be far from impracticable."[8]

Fifty of those vessels were warships, carrying 1,000 guns. The rest were merchant ships, chartered to carry to England the rich booty in New Orleans. English speculators estimated the value of cotton, sugar, Kentucky whiskey, flour, port, and other produce stored there as $15,000,000.[9] An itemized list in *Niles' Register* arrives at a larger total value.[10]

Baratarians tried but had been unable to get much produce out of the country. In 1811, Beluche had made a run to Bordeaux in

---

[7] George Robert Gleig, *A Narrative of the Campaigns of the British Army at Washington and New Orleans, under Generals Ross, Pakenham, and Lambert, in the Years 1814 and 1815* (London, 1826), 65.

[8] *A Subaltern In America: Comprising His Narrative of the Campaigns of the British Army, at Baltimore, Washington, & &, During the Late War* (Philadelphia, 1833), 187-88.

[9] Latour, *Historical Memoir*, xv; Walker, *Jackson and New Orleans*, 208.

[10] VII (February 18, 1815), 390; VIII (April 15, 1815), 113-14.

the 128-ton *Jenny*.[11] He cleared New Orleans again for Bordeaux on March 5, 1812; but the British caught him after he had crossed the Atlantic and detained him at Plymouth. This happened in May, the month before the United States declared war on Great Britain.[12] After this experience Beluche hurried back to New Orleans and accepted one of the six privateer commissions issued there by the United States.

Now, at Negril Bay, "while horses of the artillery, caught in America, were landed and turned out to pasture," Cochrane's officers were hiring all the small craft they could.[13] These would be needed in shallow coastal waters of the United States and for communication between the warships and shore.

Cochrane's armada was to transport an army such as Louisiana had never seen before. In addition to the four regiments that had vandalized from Maine to the Chesapeake, there were the four regiments Kean had brought direct from the battlefields of Europe and two regiments of Negro troops he had collected in the West Indies. These eight regiments totaled approximately 8,000 troops. The fleet would furnish 1,500 marines and 10,000 sailors.[14] Altogether, the invasion force numbered 20,000, avid for the promised "beauty and booty."[15]

Civil officers were already on board to conduct the government of Louisiana. The Honorable Mr. Elwood from Trinidad was to be lieutenant governor. A gentleman from Barbados was to be collector of the Port of New Orleans. He had with him his five, blond daughters. They were a glut on the market in Barbados, but in

---

[11] *Louisiana Gazette*, April 5, 1811.

[12] From Lloyd's List in *Louisiana Gazette*, July 21, 1812.

[13] Chesterton, *Peace, War and Adventure*, I, 167; Hill, *Recollections of an Artillery Officer*, I, 295.

[14] Latour states that after the arrival of Lambert, December 28, 1814, with 2,200 more troops, the total effective force, exclusive of sailors, was 14,450. *Historical Memoir*, Appendix No. LXIV, cxxxvi.

[15] The appetite for plunder of British troops had been whetted along the Chesapeake, in France, and in Spain. They had no reason to suppose they could not do the same in New Orleans. British prisoners and deserters reported that the "parole and countersign of the enemy's army was *beauty and booty*." Latour, *Historical Memoir*, 255-56; *Niles' Register*, VII (February 25, 1815), 410; VIII (April 22, 1815), 133.

Creole New Orleans their blond beauty would surely get them rich husbands.[16]

An attorney general, an admiralty judge and a secretary for the colony had been sent directly from England. The Superintendent of Indian Affairs had come from Canada.[17]

The list of civil officers was complete except for the choice plum. Who was to be governor of Louisiana? The man who had been shot in the neck twice by privateers. In due time he would appear. Meanwhile, officers' wives and other females with the expedition anticipated a gay season in New Orleans. They made life merry with music and dancing and other entertainment.

A government editor and printing press were part of the retinue. The editor would print and broadcast proclamations and other announcements which would explain English policy to the benighted inhabitants of New Orleans, and publish orders of the new government.

English peace commissioners at Ghent knew all this, knew that the orders of the expedition were to occupy Louisiana, ascend the Mississippi, make a junction with the 10,000 troops in Canada, and choke what was left of the United States. The invasion and occupation of Louisiana, they thought, would be easily and quickly accomplished.

---

[16] During the last part of January, 1815, Thomas Shields, Purser at the New Orleans naval station, captured some of these civil officers. They became a subject of correspondence between Master Commander Daniel T. Patterson and Admiral Cochrane. Patterson sent the whole packet, including Shields's report, to the Secretary of the Navy March 3, 1815. These are to be found in the National Archives, Naval Records. Other sources for the civil officers are Gleig, *Campaigns of the British Army*, 1826 London edition, 340, 1836 London edition, 349; Latour, *Historical Memoir*, xv; James Parton, *Life of Andrew Jackson* (3 vols., New York, 1861), II, 40; William M'Carty, *History of the American War of Eighteen Hundred and Twelve* (Philadelphia, 1816), 234; and items like the following from *Niles' Register*, VII (February 25, 1815), 411: " The Plantagenet 74 arrived at Havana a little while since . . . it is notorious that they had also with them a comptroller, collector, printing presses and apparatus, and everything else that belonged to the *permanent* establishment they originally designed to have made at New Orleans."

[17] The Indian administrator was a son of the notorious Colonel Dockstadter of Tory fame in the Revolutionary annals of the Mohawk Valley. Augustus C. Buell, *History of Andrew Jackson* (2 vols., New York, 1904), II, 72-73.

Therefore, the English peace commissioners declared to the Americans: " We do not admit of Bonaparte's construction of the law of nations. We cannot accept it in relation to the subject-matter before us." [18] This meant the Treaty of Ghent would not apply to what they called the *province* of Louisiana because they did not recognize it as belonging to the United States.

The American commissioners were uneasy. Perhaps they would have felt better had they known that watchdogs like Beluche, Dominique You, Vincent Gambie, Chighizola and others were well aware of British activity. In fact, Lieutenant George Robert Gleig of the British Eighty-fifth Regiment reported that " the West Indian seas at this time swarmed with American privateers, and it was of great consequence to keep the storeships and heavy transports in the middle of the squadron." [19]

One morning one of the privateers approached a British transport, and an officer on the transport observed that: " The decks of this vessel were crowded with a group of piratical independent-looking fellows, of all sorts of complexions. While carelessly lounging in every possible posture, some leaned over the gunwale, whilst others stood erect with arms folded or akimbo. These men wore red and striped shirts; many of their sleeves tucked above the elbows of their brawny arms; their heads cased in various colored handkerchiefs or hairy caps, and other outlandish gear; hardly one of the piratical-looking fellows wore a jacket, owing to the genial warmth of the atmosphere.

"At first they hailed us in French through a hoarse speaking trumpet, a language we pretended not to understand; they then questioned us in English. But finding that we were only a transport, they took no further notice, and ploughed through the water to reconnoitre the body of the convoy." [20]

The " piratical, independent-looking " fellows did indeed go after

---

[18] *Ibid.*, II, 75-77; Adams, *History of United States*, IX, 9-11.
[19] *Campaigns of British Army*, 1836 London edition, 215.
[20] John Henry Cooke, *A Narrative of Events in the South of France and of the Attack on New Orleans, in 1814 and 1815* (London, 1835), 190-91.

better game, the small war vessel *Volcano*. They "set more sail and ran to windward, moving just out of gunshot, in a parallel direction to us," reported Gleig who was on the *Volcano*.

It was now necessary to fall upon some plan of deceiving him, otherwise . . . he would attack. . . . The height of the bulwark served to conceal some of our men. . . . Captain Price, in order to give his ship a still greater resemblance than it already had to a merchantman, displayed an old faded scarlet ensign, and drew up his fore and mainsail in what sailors term a lubberly manner.

As yet the stranger had shown no colours, but from her build and rigging, there was little doubt as to her country. She was a beautiful schooner, presenting seven ports on a side, and apparently crowded with men,—circumstances which immediately led us to believe that she was an American privateer. The Volcano, on the other hand, was a clumsy strong-built ship, carrying twelve guns; and the Golden Fleece (the transport) mounted eight; so that, in point of artillery, the advantage was rather on our side; but the American's sailing was so much superior to that of either of us, that this advantage was more than counterbalanced.

Having dogged us till eight o'clock and reconnoitred with great exactness, the stranger began to steer gradually nearer and nearer, till at length it was judged that she had arrived within range. A gun was accordingly fired from the Volcano, and another from the transport, the balls from both of which passed over her, and fell into the sea. Finding herself thus assaulted, she instantly threw off her disguise, and hung out an American ensign; when, putting her helm up, she poured a broadside, with a volley of musquetry, into the transport; and ran alongside of the bomb (Volcano), which sailed to windward.

As soon as her flag was displayed, and her intention of attacking discerned, all hands were ordered up, and she received two well-directed broadsides from the Volcano, as well as a warm salute from the Golden Fleece. But such was the celerity of her motion, that she was alongside of the bomb in less time than can be imagined; and actually dashing her bow against the other, attempted to board. Captain Price, however, was ready to receive them. The boarders were at their posts in an instant, and the enemy discovering, when it was too late, the mistake into which he had fallen, left about twenty of his men upon the Volcano's bowsprit, all of whom were thrown into the sea; and filling his sails, sheered off with the same speed with which he had borne down. In attempting to escape, he unavoidably fell somewhat to leeward, and exposed the whole of his deck to the fire of the transport. A tremendous discharge of musketry saluted him as

(33)

he passed and it was almost laughable to witness the haste with which his crew hurried below, leaving none upon deck except such as absolutely wanted to work his vessel.

The Volcano had by this time filled, and gave chase, firing with great precision at the privateer's yards and rigging, in the hope of disabling him. But as fortune would have it, none of his important ropes or yards were cut; and we had the mortification to see him, in a few minutes, beyond our reach.[21]

The Baratarians had friends on the coast of all the West Indian islands and these quickly reported any rumors or facts; so Cochrane's destination, which was supposed to be a profound secret, was soon known to the Baratarians. As one artillery officer complained: " The negociations made by the admiral for the hire of small craft," was the way in which " many persons who ought to have remained in ignorance were aware that New Orleans was the intended scene of action." [22]

The subaltern had another explanation of how the secret became known. He said: " I believe the truth to be as follows. The conquest of New Orleans was from the first the grand object . . . and so anxious were ministers to effect this, that though a general rendezvous at Jamaica, of the invading army, had been long planned out, not a hint of the matter was dropped to the naval officer commanding there, till the forces, both from England and the Potomac, were ready to set sail.

" It unhappily occurred, however, that in the interval, the Admiral on the Jamaica station died, and the dispatches designed for him were necessarily put into the hands of the senior captain. That gentleman, with a singular absence of all common prudence, opened these dispatches in the presence of a Jew merchant; and, like a perfect simpleton, informed him of their contents. . . . He fitted out a fast sailing schooner without delay, and dispatched them to the enemy." [23]

Some of the Baratarians had also been watching the British infiltration under Colonel Nicholls at Pensacola and along the

---

[21] Gleig, *Campaigns of British Army*, 1836 London edition, 220-22.
[22] Hill, *Recollections of an Artillery Officer*, I, 295.
[23] *A Subaltern in America*, 1833 Philadelphia edition, 187-88.

Florida coast. Nicholls had been successful in getting an alliance with the Creek Indians. They were smarting from their recent chastisement at the hands of Andrew Jackson. Now they would get even with " Old Sharp Knife " who had forced them to sign a treaty whereby they ceded to the United States 23,000,000 acres in Georgia and Alabama.[24] The British high command counted greatly on the aid of the Creeks. Lord Bathurst wrote in his instructions from England: " With their favor and cooperation . . . we may expect to rescue the whole province of Louisiana from the United States." [25]

It may have been Renato Beluche who sent an anonymous report on this sector to Jean Laffite. Beluche was the most literate of the Baratarians, and this letter is in the same style as hundreds of his in Archives at Bogotá. Moreover, the mayor of Pensacola was his brother-in-law.[26] This report, dated from Havana, August 8, 1814, was as follows:

Dear Sir

I embrace the opportunity offered for Pensacola, to inform you, that an expedition has sailed from Bermuda for Mobile, who touched and left this on the 11th instant, under the command of colonel Nicholls of the artillery, a brave officer well known in the European wars.

They touched here for aid in gun-boats, small vessels, &c. and for leave to land at Pensacola, all of which were refused by the captain-general. However, I learn that they are determined to land at Pensacola with or without leave, where they will embark their park of artillery. The colonel was conveyed with his troops in two sloops of war, the Hermes, commanded by the hon. W. H. Percy, and the Caron, commanded by the hon. P. Spencer, who, with such vessels as may be on the station, will cooperate with the land forces.

The brig Orpheus, some time past, landed arms and some officers at Apalachicola to arrange with the Creek nation for future operations against Mobile, New Orleans and that district of the country, which they effected, and caused the breaking off the treaty.

The whole nation are ready to join the British troops under colonel

---

[24] Marquis James, *Andrew Jackson The Border Captain* (Indianapolis, 1933), 187-90.
[25] Bathurst to Ross, September 28, 1814; MSS in the British Archives, cited in Adams, *History of United States*, VIII, 313.
[26] *AGI, PdeC, Legajo* 1874, cited in Faye, " Privateersmen of the Gulf," 16 in the reprint.

Nicholls, who will immediately on his arrival issue his proclamation, declaring all slaves who will join their standard free and liberated forever from their masters. He will also issue another to the Indians, promising all the tribes who will join him, to reinstate them in all their lands taken from them by the United States, and to guarantee the same to them forever. Having thus prepared the minds of the negroes and Indians, he will on arrival of two or three black regiments from Nassau, &c. of fine troops, calculated for that climate (who may pass by this next week) push for New Orleans—first having secured and fortified Mobile point, and taken Mobile, as well as placed a force at every point on the lakes, of any importance, as well as Plaquemines in order to cut off all trade of the Mississippi.

This force with him is small, but he will soon be re-enforced from Bermuda, &c.—the flying artillery appears well calculated for his operations in that country.[27]

Jean Laffite was well informed when he was approached by agents from Colonel Nicholls.

---

[27] Latour, *Historical Memoir*, Appendix No. 2, v-vi.

THE BRITISH APPROACH

JEAN LAFFITE

EARLY ON THE MORNING OF SEPTEMBER 3, 1814, GRANDE TERRE was aroused by a cannon shot coming from the direction of the Gulf. Two hundred Baratarians ran to see what was up. A British sloop had fired a gun at one of their ships about to enter the Pass and had forced her to run aground. The sloop anchored at the entrance.

Four Baratarians quickly manned a boat and rowed Jean Laffite to the scene.[1] A tender bearing British colors and a flag of truce came toward them. Captain Nicholas Lockyer, commander of the sloop, and Captain McWilliams of the army were in the tender.

"Is Mr. Laffite at home in the bay? I have important communications for him," said Captain Lockyer.

"You will have to come to shore if you want to see Mr. Laffite," replied Jean. "Follow me," he added, and the boats rode through the Pass and into the harbor.

Two hundred glowering Baratarians watched every move. Now the Englishmen were in Jean Laffite's power. "I am Jean Laffite," he said.

Captain McWilliams handed him a packet addressed to "Mr. Laffite—Barataria."

---

[1] USDC of La., Case No. 746, testimony of E. Williams.

"Make them prisoners," growled the Baratarians.

"You had better come into my house while we discuss this matter," Jean said to the Englishmen. Then he turned to the Baratarians saying, "These men have come under a flag of truce. We must respect it."

"They're spies! They have come to spy out the coast so they can invade and plunder the country," was the general cry. "We should make them prisoners and send them to New Orleans."

"Let me talk to them first and find out what is in the papers. You can keep guard to see that there is no communication with the sloop until I am through," answered Jean.[2]

The surly mob agreed and Jean led the Englishmen to his headquarters. He broke the seal on the first communication. It was Colonel Nicholls' proclamation to the citizens of Louisiana and it said:

Natives of Louisiana! On you the first call is made to assist in liberating from a faithless, imbecile government, your paternal soil. Spaniards, Frenchmen, Italians, and British, . . . on you I call to aid me in this just cause. The American usurpation in this country must be abolished, and the lawful owners of the soil put in possession.

I am at the head of a large body of Indians, well armed, disciplined, and commanded by British officers—a good train of artillery with every requisite, seconded by the powerful aid of a numerous British and Spanish squadron of ships and vessels of war.

Be not alarmed, inhabitants of the country, at our approach. The same good faith and disinterestedness which has distinguished the conduct of Britons in Europe accompanies them here. You will have no fear of litigious taxes imposed on you for the purpose of carrying on an unnatural and unjust war; your property, your laws, the peace and tranquility of your country will be guaranteed to you by men who will suffer no infringement of theirs. Rest assured that these brave red men only burn with an ardent desire of satisfaction for the wrongs they have suffered from Americans, to join you in liberating these southern provinces from their yoke and drive them into the limits formerly prescribed by my sovereign.

The Indians have pledged themselves, in the most solemn manner, not

---

[2] This conversation is based on such accounts as Latour, *Historical Memoir*, 17-18; and Walker, *Jackson and New Orleans*, 40-43.

to injure in the slightest degree, the persons or properties of any but enemies.[3]

As Jean Laffite read this proclamation, not a muscle of his face moved. The Englishmen had not the slightest hint of his reaction. Jean reached for the second document—a letter from William H. Percy, Captain and Senior Officer in the Gulf of Mexico. It said:

Having understood that some British merchantmen have been detained, taken into, and sold by the inhabitants of Barataria, I have directed Captain Lockyer, of His Majesty's sloop *Sophia*, to proceed to that place and inquire into the circumstances with positive orders to demand instant restitution and, in case of refusal, to destroy to his utmost every vessel there, as well as to carry destruction over the whole place, and at the same time to assure him of the co-operation of all His Majesty's naval force on this station.

I trust at the same time that the inhabitants of Barataria, consulting their own interests, will not make it necessary to proceed to such extremities—I hold out at the same time a war instantly destructive to them; and, on the other hand, should they be inclined to assist Great Britain in her just and unprovoked war against the United States, the security of their property, the blessings of the British Constitution—and should they be inclined to settle on this continent, lands will, at the conclusion of the war, be allotted them in His Majesty's colonies in America. In return for all these concessions on the part of Great Britain I expect that the directions of their armed vessels will be put into my hands (for which they will be remunerated), the instant cessation of hostilities against the Spanish government, and the restitution of any undisposed property of that nation. . . .[4]

"In this letter," said Jean, "Great Britain threatens to destroy Barataria unless we help her invade the United States. If we do help, my men are to be considered British subjects and will be rewarded with lands taken from the Americans; but what will my reward be?"

"The Governor of Louisiana has declared you and your men to be outlaws," answered Captain Lockyer. "Your brother Pierre is

---

[3] Latour, *Historical Memoir*, Appendix No. III, vii-viii. This proclamation has been quoted by many authors. The original is in Bibliotheca Parsoniana: La.-Am. MSS, No. 1023.

[4] *Ibid.*, Appendix No. III, ix-x; Bibliotheca Parsoniana: La.-Am. MSS, No. 1024.

at this very moment loaded with irons in the jail of New Orleans.[5] We will free your brother. Moreover, you will receive a reward of $30,000 and be made a captain in the British service. This will mean a great career before you in England's new colony. Do not let slip this opportunity of acquiring fortune and consideration." [6]

Thirty thousand dollars—what a paltry bribe to offer Jean Laffite. At that very moment his thatched-roof warehouses on Grande Terre alone were bursting with prize goods worth more than a million dollars.

"You saw how ominous my men were when you came in," Jean answered calmly. "I will need a little time to persuade them to accept this offer. But first, let us dine."

The amazed Englishmen soon found themselves drinking choice wines and eating exotic foods served with elegance on silver plates and priceless damask. Jean persuaded them to be his guests for the night. Actually, they were his prisoners.

---

[5] Writs were still out against Jean and Pierre Laffite when Pierre brazenly showed himself in the streets of New Orleans. So the Marshal could certify on July 8, 1814, that he had "committed Pierre Laffite to prison for want of bail."

It was at this time that Grymes resigned as district attorney to become Pierre's lawyer. However, he was unable to get him out of the Cabildo. In August he petitioned the Court to have a physician make an inquiry into the state of the prisoner's health "and to report on the expediency of relieving him of irons in his confinement." Drs. William Flood and Lewis Heermann "in compliance with the directions of the Honorable Dominique A. Hall" examined Pierre and reported:

That said Pierre Laffite appears to have suffered about two years ago an apoplectic fit succeeded by palsy of the left side and that he is habitually subject to paroxysms resembling hysteria.

We further report that the said Laffite is at present entirely free from any symptoms indicating the probability of an early return of apoplexy, and that lowness of spirit from agitation of mind appears to be the only indisposition he labors under.

With due regard, therefore, to every indulgence of a prisoner, we are of the opinion that there is no apparent necessity of relieving him of irons which have been applied, as a means of security; and as far as may be consistent with safety, we would beg leave to recommend that he should be reasonably indulged in taking as much exercise as his confinement within the walls of the jail will admit of.

Lewis Heermann
Wm Flood

August 10, 1814
USDC of La., Case No. 574.

[6] Latour, *Historical Memoir*, 19.

Later, Jean consulted with his captains. The next morning Baratarians surrounded the house and made threatening demonstrations. Jean told the Engishmen that they had better go back to their ship while he calmed the Baratarians. " You will have my answer within a very short time," he assured them.

True to his word, Jean sent Captain Lockyer his answer. It was written in French and said:

Sir

The confusion which prevailed in our camp yesterday and this morning, and of which you have a complete knowledge, has prevented me from answering in a precise manner to the object of your mission: not even at this moment can I give you all the satisfaction that you desire; however, if you grant me a fortnight, I would be entirely at your disposal at the end of that time—this delay is indispensable to send away the three persons who have alone occasioned all the disturbance—the two who were the most troublesome are to leave this place in eight days, and the other is to go to town—the remainder of the time is necessary to enable me to put my affairs in order—you may communicate with me, by sending a boat to the eastern point of the pass, where I will be found. You have inspired me with more confidence than the admiral, your superior officer, could have done himself; with you alone I wish to deal, and from you also I will claim, in due time, the reward for the services which I may render to you.

Be so good, sir, as to favour me with an answer, and believe me yours, &c.

Laffite [7]

Jean and his captains held a consultation. They decided to send all the communications from the British to Jean Blanque, who had come to Louisiana in 1803 with his cousin Pierre Clément Laussat, whom Napoleon had sent as his prefect. Jean Blanque was not only the owner of a number of ships the Baratarians sailed; he was also a member of the legislature and a man of influence in New Orleans. " It was impossible to hear him without remembering all that he had said, so correct was he. In habitual commerce with men he was patient, kind, human and serviceable. After being received as a lawyer at the bar, he pleaded without remuneration," [8] In a country

[7] Bibliotheca Parsoniana: La.-Am. MSS, No. 1031.
[8] Blanque was married to Delphine Macarty, widow of Don Ramón López y Angula,

where the power of the word dominated, the Baratarians could not have selected a better champion. Laffite sent this explanation to Jean Blanque:

> Though proscribed by my adoptive country, I will never let slip an occasion of serving her, or of proving that she has never ceased to be dear to me. Of this you will here see a convincing proof. Yesterday, the 3rd of September, there appeared here, under a flag of truce, a boat coming from an English brig, at anchor about two leagues from the pass. Mr. Nicholas Lockyer, a British officer of high rank, delivered me the following papers: two directed to me, a proclamation, and the admiral's instructions to Captain Lockyer; all herewith inclosed. . . . I make you the depository of the secret on which perhaps depends the tranquility of our country; please to make such use of it as your judgment may direct.
>
> Our enemies have endeavoured to work on me by a motive which few men would have resisted. They represented to me a brother in irons, a brother who is very dear to me, whose deliverer I might become, and I declined the proposal. . . . I have asked fifteen days to settle my affairs, assigning such plausible pretexts, that I hope the term will be granted. I am waiting for the British officer's answer, and for yours to this. Be so good as to assist me with your judicious counsel in so weighty an affair.[9]

When Laffite had finished this letter, he sent for Raymond Ranchier, his swiftest messenger, and gave the packet to him to deliver.[10] Ranchier travelled by " courier pirogue." Ten husky slaves rowed him across Barataria Bay and through the lakes. They were relieved by the next relay which took Ranchier past The Temple and up Bayou Barataria to its head, where he got on a horse and galloped to the river. A waiting pirogue ferried him across the

---

Consul General for Spain. Blanque's " stature was above the ordinary. He was well made. His face was oval; his beard and his fine eyes black; his nose aquiline; his manners were the manners of a son of good family who had never ceased to frequent good society. Add to all that, he was always ready to draw sword or pistol. His diction was remarkable in spite of a Southern accent. His oxordium invited a hearing. His narration was clear and connected. His peroration warm and filled with metaphors." Typescript translation of Bernard de Marigny, *Reflection on the Campaign of General Andrew Jackson, in Louisiana 1814 and 1815* (New Orleans: W.P.A., 1938), 18-19; originally published in French by J. L. Sollée (New Orleans, 1848).

[9] Bibliotheca Parsoniana: La.-Am. MSS, No. 1022.
[10] *Journal of Jean Laffite*, 47.

Mississippi, and Ranchier appeared before Jean Blanque 24 hours after he left Grande Terre.[11] This trip normally took three days.

Jean Blanque read the letters and immediately took the packet to Governor Claiborne. " I must confer with a committee of the legislature," said Claiborne.

This committee soon assembled. Some of the members were Major Jacques Villeré, commander of the Louisiana Militia; Commodore Daniel T. Patterson of the United States Navy; [12] Colonel George Ross, commanding the 44th United States Infantry; and Pierre Du Bourg, Collector of United States Customs. Claiborne presented the letters. They were read. Then the governor said: " The council must decide two questions: first, are these letters genuine; second, is it proper for the Governor of Louisiana to enter into any correspondence with Jean Laffite or any of his associates? " [13]

One member of the committee sprang to his feet and cried, " These letters are a ruse on the part of Jean Laffite to get Pierre out of jail and make us look ridiculous."

Commodore Patterson spoke up and said, " My instructions from the Secretary of the Navy are to disperse the Baratarian association. The schooner *Carolina* has been sent here for that purpose. Colonel Ross and I have made preparations to carry out these instructions." [14]

Colonel Ross told the committee that his instructions were to cooperate with Commodore Patterson; and Collector Du Bourg shouted, " The smugglers' stronghold should be attacked and destroyed, now! [15]

Only one member spoke in defense of the Baratarians. "I know them," said Major Villeré. " They are not pirates, they are privateers. Their ships sail under the flag of Cartagena. They can not bring their

---

[11] Arthur, *Jean Laffite*, 65.

[12] Patterson's rank was master commander, one grade lower than a naval captain. The rank of commodore was not created in America until 1862, and is a grade higher than that of captain. Jackson and other contemporaries of Patterson called him " commodore." John Spencer Bassett, *The Life of Andrew Jackson* (New York, 1925), 165.

[13] Latour, *Historical Memoir*, 253.

[14] *Ibid.*

[15] *Ibid.*; Arthur, *Jean Laffite*, 73.

prizes into our ports legally. The only crime which can be charged against them is that they have disposed of their prize goods by illegal means. The United States is their adopted country. They see it threatened by an enemy they hate. These documents are true. We must believe the Baratarians." [16]

But Major Villeré was "a voice crying in the wilderness." Claiborne paid no heed to him. True, the governor did not vote but neither did he speak in behalf of the Baratarians. Claiborne was a transplanted Virginia politician who had swung the Tennessee vote for Jefferson in the presidential election of 1800. As a reward he had been sent to the Spanish frontier to govern Louisiana. He had been on that frontier ten years, long enough to develop frontier instincts. But perhaps because the Laffites had wounded his vanity and perhaps because of the importunities of his Spanish wife and her people, Claiborne was blind when opportunity knocked at his door. He missed greatness because he did not champion the Baratarians. Instead, he let the committee decide what should be done and he abided by that decision.

The committee, with Major Villeré dissenting, decided the letters were a ruse to get Pierre out of jail. Commodore Patterson was directed to carry out the mission for which he had been sent to Louisiana—destroy the Barataria establishment on Grande Terre.

Meanwhile, Laffite's friends and perhaps even J. H. Holland, the jailor, managed Pierre's escape from the Cabildo so that Pierre returned to Grande Terre with Jules Ranchier.[17] The next day Holland put a notice in the papers and placed posters throughout New Orleans stating that:

1000 Dollars Reward

Will be paid to whoever arrests Pierre Laffite, who last night, broke from the parish prison and escaped. The said Pierre Laffite is five feet, ten inches tall, and of robust stature, light complexion, and somewhat

---

[16] Latour, *Historical Memoir*, 254; Walker, *Jackson and New Orleans*, 45; Francois Xavier Martin, *The History of Louisiana* (2 vols., New Orleans, 1827-29), II, 239.
[17] Arthur, *Jean Laffite*, 71. Jules Ranchier in *The Journal of Jean Laffite* is cited as Raymond Ranchier.

cross-eyed. It is believed that a more complete description of the said Laffite is useless as he is so well known in this city.[18]

This was not only to cover up his own action in the escape, but Holland's way of informing the Creoles. When Pierre arrived at Grande Terre with Ranchier, Jean was worried about the effect of the escape on Claiborne. He wrote to the governor the best letter he ever composed. One can feel his concern in the unusual deference to Claiborne as one reads the letter which was as follows:

Grande Terre, 10 September, 1814

A Son Excellence Monsieur
Wm. C. C. Claiborne, Gouverneur
de l'Etat de la Louisiane;

Monsieur—

In the firm persuasion that the choice made of you to fill the office of first magistrate was dictated by the esteem of your fellow citizens and was conferred on merit, I confidently address you on an affair on which may depend the safety of this country.

I offer to you to restore to this state several citizens who, perhaps in your eyes, have lost that sacred title. I offer you them, however, such as you could wish to find them, ready to exert their utmost efforts in defense of the country. This point of Louisiana which I occupy, is of great importance in the present crisis. I tender my services to defend it and the only reward I ask is that a stop be put to the proscription against me and my adherents, by an act of oblivion for all that has been done hitherto.

I am the stray sheep wishing to return to the flock. If you were thoroughly acquainted with the nature of my offenses I should appear to you much less guilty and still worthy to discharge the duties of a good citizen. I have never sailed under any flag but that of the republic of Carthagena, and my vessels are perfectly regular in that respect. If I could have brought my lawful prizes into the ports of this state, I should not have employed the illicit means that have caused me to be proscribed.

I decline saying more on the subject until I have the honour of your excellency's answer, which I am persuaded can be dictated only by wisdom.

In case, Monsieur le Gouverneur, your reply should not be favourable to my ardent wishes I declare to you that I will leave so as not to be held

---

[18] *Louisiana Courier*, September 7, 9, 12, 28, 1814.

to have co-operated with an invasion on this point, which cannot fail to take place, and puts me entirely at the judgment of my conscience.

> Jai l'Honneru d'etre,
> M. le Gouverneur
> Jn Laffite [19]

After dispatching Ranchier to New Orleans with this letter, Jean supervised the transfer of arms and ammunition stored on Grande Terre to warehouses hidden in the vicinity of The Temple. The slaves in the barracoons were sent elsewhere. Then several ships were loaded with important papers, maps Jean had collected, hard money, and the most valuable merchandise. Jean expected the British would be vindictive when they learned he had been stalling for time, so none of those things which might help the enemy were left on the island. The two weeks he had asked for were almost gone when Jean sailed with his loaded vessels to Isle Dernière, about forty miles west of Grande Terre. Pierre was ill. He traveled by pirogue to a plantation on Bayou Lafourche to convalesce.[20]

Dominique You was left in charge at Grande Terre. If the British attacked he was to bombard them from the fort at the Pass and set fire to warehouses and whatever ships were in the harbor. Many writers assume that Renato Beluche was with Dominique at this time and he may have been.

Meanwhile, Commodore Patterson was sailing down the Mississippi with six gunboats, one launch, and the *Carolina*, equipped for battle and carrying part of the 44th Regiment.[21]

On the morning of September 16, Dominique's sentinels sighted Patterson's squadron approaching. Dominique was expecting the British. His cannon were ready to fire. When the vessels were close enough so that he could make out the flag, Dominique stopped short. He could not fire on the flag of the United States. Instead, he ordered his men to set fire to the warehouses and the ships.

From the *Carolina* Patterson could see the action on Grande Terre.

---

[19] Stanley Arthur's translation, *Jean Laffite*, 71-72.
[20] Latour, *Historical Memoir*, 254.
[21] USDC of La., Case No. 734.

" I perceived that the pirates were abandoning their vessels and were flying in all directions," he testified later in court.[22]

About 500 Baratarians did escape before Patterson landed and took possession of the ships and the island. Dominique surrendered. He and 80 Baratarians were made prisoners. Patterson did not have 100m for any more. He and his men spent the next four days loading the 26 captured vessels and their transports with the loot they rescued from burning warehouses.[23]

On Patterson's last day at Grande Terre, one of Beluche's vessels approached the island. It was the *General Bolívar* arriving from Cartagena. The captain at this time, according to the ship's papers, was Joseph Clement. He could not know what had been going on in Barataria Bay, but he did see a strange ship lying outside the Pass. The strange ship was the *Carolina*. Her commander sighted the *General Bolívar* and immediately gave the signal to chase.

Clement altered the course of the *General Bolívar*, firing several shots at the pursuing vessel. " The Carolina gaining fast, the General Bolivar changed its course again and bore away for Grande Terre. The Carolina hoisted her colors and continued to fire until the General Bolivar was grounded." Clement and his crew " immediately abandoned ship and got on shore and disappeared." The commanding officer of the *Carolina* " did thereupon seize and take possession of the General Bolivar with her apparel, guns and appurtenances and therein departed therewith " for New Orleans.[24]

Patterson reported to the Secretary of the Navy his regret that the Baratarians had not fought him. " But," he added, " it is a great subject of satisfaction to me to have effected the object of my enterprise; viz. capturing all their vessels in port, and dispersing their band without having one of my brave fellows hurt. The enemy had mounted on their vessels twenty pieces of cannon of different calibre. . . ." [25]

---

[22] *Ibid.*, Case No. 760.

[23] Arthur gives the names of the captured vessels. His list is accurate; it was compiled from federal court records. *Jean Laffite*, 87-88.

[24] USDC of La., Case No. 760.

[25] *Historical Military Data, Louisiana Militia 1811-1814* (Jackson Barracks, New Orleans, 1941).

When Patterson and his flotilla reached New Orleans, he charged the Baratarians with piracy and they were jailed in the Cabildo. Dominique You was chained to heavy irons. Then Patterson filed suit for himself and his men, claiming the vessels and stores seized at Grande Terre.[26]

However, it was not long before plaintiffs and defendants suspended the suit to deal with a common enemy.

---

[26] Private letters said the goods captured by Patterson at Barataria were worth $500,000. *Niles' Register*, VII (October 27, 1814), 111. Jean Laffite says the value was $600,000. *Journal*, 54.

ANDREW JACKSON

DURING 1813 AND 1814 ANDREW JACKSON MADE HOSTILE CREEKS on the Florida frontier wish they had never heard of him. By the summer of 1814 they were ready to make peace.

At this point William Henry Harrison resigned from the United States Army. The powers that controlled promotions dared not give the vacant commission to any one but "Old Hickory." So he was made commander of Military District No. 7. This included the states of Tennessee and Louisiana and the Mississippi Territory. Headquarters for this district were at Mobile, since Jackson's main duty would be to protect the Gulf coast.

Jackson did not proceed to Mobile until after the Creeks had signed the treaty whereby they ceded what is today one-fifth of the state of Georgia and three-fifths of Alabama to the United States. This area was added to Jackson's command.

The Secretary of War had assigned five regiments of the United States Infantry to the defense of this district. They were the Second, Third, Seventh, Thirty-ninth and Forty-fourth. They totalled 2,378 men. The Seventh and Forty-fourth were mostly Creoles from Louisiana.[1]

Jackson left central Alabama on August 11, and going down the

---

[1] Marigny, *Reflection on the Campaign*, 13.

ANDREW JACKSON.

river of that name, reached Mobile on August 15. Two large river systems empty into Mobile Bay—the Alabama and the Tombigbee. If the English should get into the bay, they could penetrate the United States for hundreds of miles up these rivers and their tributaries.

Thirty miles across the bay from Mobile was Fort Bowyer. It was on a narrow, sandy peninsula that almost closed Mobile Bay from the Gulf of Mexico. Fort Bowyer, on the tip of this peninsula, controlled the narrow entrance to the bay from the Gulf.

Jackson found Fort Bowyer abandoned!

He sent Major William Lawrence with 160 men, all he could spare, to repair the fort and strengthen its defenses. Lawrence and his men worked like Trojans. They found twenty cannon which they remounted. While they worked, the British burned Washington, raided the Chesapeake, then dispatched vessels to the West Indies to collect black troops, and extend their beachheads at Pensacola and Apalachicola.

As Jackson entered the critical theater of war operations against Great Britain, he could get no help from Washington. United States government officials fled while the city burned. When the Secretary of War finally sent dispatches to Jackson, they did not arrive until after the war was over. The same was true of supplies. A government contractor was supposed to bring some from Pittsburgh down the Ohio and the Mississippi, but he did not get to New Orleans until two months after the war was over.

Jackson knew within 48 hours after arriving at Mobile that the English at Pensacola, 60 miles away, had landed marines, seized the city, and were recruiting Creek Indians. Western and Southern newspapers raged about the assistance the Spanish governor of Pensacola was giving the British.

" Old Hickory " wanted to go right after the British and drive them from Florida but he could not. He did not have enough troops. He had to send to Tennessee, Kentucky (this state was outside his jurisdiction), and the Mississippi Territory for them and *wait* two months until they arrived.

(51)

Meanwhile, the *Sophie* which Sir William H. Percy had sent with dispatches to Jean Laffite returned to Pensacola. Percy decided to attack Mobile without waiting to see whether or not Jean Laffite and his men would aid the British. He boasted that he would make the fort surrender within twenty minutes.[2]

So it happened that on the morning of September 12, 1814, an outpost at Fort Bowyer reported the British had landed marines and Indians a few miles east of the fort. That evening the little garrison saw four British war vessels anchor six miles from them.

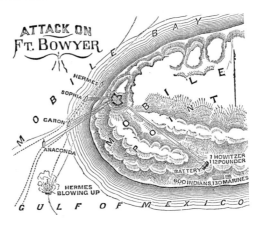

Two days later, at 4:30, the *Hermes* ran broadside into the channel and dropped anchor within musket shot of the fort. The rest of the ships followed and anchored one behind the other. Then a thundering cannonade burst from enemy guns. It was answered by only 12 of Fort Bowyer's 20 guns. Eight were not in position to use.

Marines and Indians opened fire behind a bluff. A few shots from the south battery silenced them and kept them away. Colonel Nicholls lost an eye when a splinter lodged in it.[3]

A lucky shot from the fort cut the cable of the *Hermes*. The current turned her bow to the fort and for twenty minutes a terrible

---

[2] Adams, *History of United States*, VIII, 323; Latour, *Historical Memoir*, 39-41; Buell, *History of Andrew Jackson*, I, 344.

[3] Washington *Daily National Intelligencer*, October 15, 1814.

fire raked her from stem to stern. Then she ran aground. Commander Percy transferred his wounded to the *Sophie*, set fire to the *Hermes*, and abandoned her.

Then Sir William H. Percy, minus one ship, and Colonel Edward Nicholls, minus one eye, proceeded to Pensacola. Two marines deserted. They told Major Lawrence the British casualties were 162 killed and 70 wounded, including Colonel Nicholls.[4]

Major Lawrence took stock. Four dead in the fort, four wounded in battle and six when some cartridges burst. Seven hundred cannon balls had been shot, two guns had been knocked off their carriages, four cracked beyond repair; and three hundred holes had been made in the fort.[5]

Because the British had not taken Fort Bowyer, they determined to bypass Mobile. Their instructions said to occupy the *province* of Louisiana by advancing directly on New Orleans, or move into the back parts of Georgia and the country of friendly Indians. They decided to make a direct approach to New Orleans.

At that moment Jean Laffite and his Baratarians were contributing to the security of the United States by refusing to guide the English through bayous west of the Mississippi. A glance at the map will show that the easiest access to New Orleans from the Gulf is up Bayou Lafourche or through the bays and bayous of Barataria. If Jean Laffite had sided with the enemy, British troops could have moved easily and rapidly to a point above New Orleans. Then the city could have been cut off from all communication with the interior.

Convinced that the Baratarians had tricked them, and afraid of a possible trap, the British abandoned all idea of including Barataria in their theater of operations. Without Laffite's small ships they could not navigate the bayous even though they could find their way.

So the British top command narrowed the field of operation and eliminated the best approach to New Orleans. The only one left was from below the city: up the Mississippi itself, which meant bucking 120 miles of currents and curves, to say nothing of winds

---

[4] Latour, *Historical Memoir*, 40; Adams, *History of United States*, VIII, 323-24.
[5] Parton, *Life of Jackson*, I, 608.

and calms, or through some bayou that emptied into Lake Borgne and the Gulf.

After the British were defeated at Fort Bowyer, Jackson received Jean Laffite's packet of letters which Claiborne had forwarded to him. Jackson read Colonel Nicholls' "Proclamation to Louisianians" and one can almost see "Old Hickory" rushing to broadcast a proclamation also. It said:

> Louisianians!
>
> The base, perfidious Britons have attempted to invade your country— they had the temerity to attack fort Bowyer with their incongruous horde of Indians and negro assassins—they seem to have forgotten that this fort was defended by freemen—they were not long indulged in their error—the gallant Lawrence, with his little spartan band, has given them a lecture that will last for ages; he has taught them what men can do when fighting for their liberty, when contending against slaves. He has convinced Sir W. H. Percy that his companions in arms were not to be conquered by proclamations; that the strongest British bark is not invulnerable to the force of American artillery, directed by the steady nervous arm of a freeman.
>
> Louisianians! The proud Briton, the natural and sworn Enemy of all Frenchmen, has called upon you, by proclamation, to aid him in his tyranny, and to prostrate the holy temple of our liberty. Can Louisianians, can Frenchmen, can Americans, ever stoop to be the slaves or allies of Britain?

Then Jackson pounced upon the British offer to the Baratarians as he continued:

> I ask you, Louisianians, can we place any confidence in the honour of men who have courted an alliance with pirates and robbers? Have not these noble Britons, these honourable men, colonel Nicholls and the honourable captain W. H. Percy, the true representatives of their royal master, done this? Have they not made offers to the pirates of Barataria to join them, and their holy cause? And have they not dared to insult you by calling on you to associate, as brethren with them, and this hellish banditti.[6]

"Hellish banditti"—that was what Jackson thought of the Bara-

---

[6] John Spencer Bassett (ed.), *Correspondence of Andrew Jackson* (7 vols., Washington, 1926-35), II, 57-58.

tarians. He self-righteously ignored them. He did not know then that Jean Laffite and his Baratarians had contributed greatly to the security of the United States by refusing to cooperate with the British.

Jackson was worried, fussing and fuming while waiting for the volunteers from Kentucky, Tennessee, and Mississippi. Six inactive weeks he waited. His dysentery got worse and his body wasted to skin and bone, but nothing could conquer the indomitable spirit that gleamed from his cadaverous eyes.

General John Coffee with 1,800 Tennesseans arrived first, then Thomas Hinds and his Mississippi mounted rifles, about a hundred and fifty strong. These, with his seven hundred regulars, a hundred or more volunteers from Mobile and Captain Pierre Jugeat with his two hundred and fifty Choctaws gave Jackson a grand total of 3,000 troops. Early in November he distributed rations for eight days and marched his troops to Pensacola. When he prepared to storm the city it surrendered.

The British held Fort Barrancas, 14 miles away at the mouth of the bay. The Spanish governor, González, sent them a written order to surrender, that Jackson and his men would take command the next day.

That night the British blew up Fort Barrancas and departed. They left disillusioned Spaniards and Indians behind. Where had they gone? Back to mutilated Fort Bowyer to capture Mobile while Jackson was absent with his troops?

Jackson evacuated Pensacola and dashed to Mobile. He saw no sign of the British but heard increasing rumors of the invasion fleet. "Old Hickory" waited 11 days at Mobile and still no sign of the British. Then he thought he had better look into the situation at New Orleans. He did not think the British would be so foolhardy as to attack New Orleans directly, but they might.

Jackson's " Proclamation " and other sources had made known the contents of Laffite's letters and the people of New Orleans had become panicky. Livingston and Governor Claiborne had been writing Jackson, describing the defenseless city and urging him to come. The legislature was wasting time in endless debate. The

Creole faction, on general principles, blocked every move Governor Claiborne's supporters tried to make.

The legislature had appointed a defense committee to work with Claiborne and Commodore Patterson, but concerted action was frustrated not only by personal jealousies, but by another defense committee. Citizens, having no confidence in the governor nor in the legislature, had appointed their own defense committee. Livingston was chairman. The two defense committees worked at cross purposes with each other.

Creoles could not believe that the recently arrived Americans loved New Orleans enough to risk their lives in its defense. Their bulging warehouses represented great wealth. Surely the yankee owners would make a bargain with the enemy to preserve this treasure. English and Spanish agents raised a crop of subversive rumors that added to the general suspicion and undermined confidence.

Claiborne himself helped to maintain the feeling of panic. His correspondence during the nine months preceding the British invasion seemed to be preparing the President of the United States and his cabinet for the possibility of losing Louisiana. He reported rumors of " design on the part of the enemy to wrest Louisiana from the hands of the United States and restore it to Spain! "

Claiborne teetered back and forth between confidence in the free people of color and fear of them. When Jackson issued his " Proclamation to Louisianians," he issued one also to the free colored inhabitants of Louisiana in which he said:

> Through a mistaken policy you have heretofore been deprived of a participation in the glorious struggle for national rights in which our country is engaged. This no longer shall exist.
>
> As sons of freedom, you are now called upon to defend our most inestimable blessing. . . .
>
> To every noble-hearted, generous freeman of colour, volunteering to serve during the present contest with Great Britain, and no longer, there will be paid the same bounty in money and lands, now received by the white soldiers of the United States (viz. one hundred and twenty-four dollars in money, and one hundred and sixty acres of land). The non-commissioned

officers and privates will also be entitled to the same monthly pay and daily rations, and clothes furnished to any American soldier.[7]

This proclamation was sent to Claiborne. He did nothing about it for a whole month. On October 17, he wrote to Jackson: " The publication of your address to the free people of color is delayed a few days. An unfortunate misunderstanding between the officers of the battalion of color, which excites much interest, is the subject of investigation before a court of inquiry now sitting." [8]

So Claiborne did nothing constructive. He wrote down all the alibis that would excuse defeat and put himself in a position to be accepted by whichever side won. The difference between Jackson and Claiborne was that Jackson had made up his mind to defeat the British and he did not waste any energy inventing excuses for failure. Instead of deprecating the free men of color as a source of strength, Jackson was determined to use them. But before he went to New Orleans to clear up the mess there and organize the city for defense, Jackson moved to their stations the men on his half of the checkerboard of war.

He sent one thousand Tennessee horsemen to scour the Florida coast and keep the English from making a beachhead there. Major Lawrence and his valiants were to remain at Fort Bowyer, while three regiments of regulars (2nd, 3rd, 39th) were kept at Mobile. This was the main body of Jackson's force, but surely the British would try again to take Mobile and penetrate to Baton Rouge. General Coffee was sent with twelve hundred mounted troops to Baton Rouge, to protect New Orleans from a possible British break-through and attack from above. The Seventh Regiment joined the Forty-fourth at New Orleans.

Meanwhile, Jackson had sent messengers to Kentucky, Tennessee, and Mississippi, pleading for more volunteers and urging them to hasten to New Orleans. On the 22nd of November, he put his dysentery-wracked body on a horse and travelled by land, 125 miles, to have firsthand knowledge of points at which the enemy might

---

[7] Latour, *Historical Memoir*, Appendix No. XVII, xxxi-xxxii.
[8] Gayarré, *History of Louisiana*, IV, 365-66.

effect a landing. When he was halfway to New Orleans, Cochrane's invasion fleet left Negril Bay, Jamaica; and as Jackson entered the city of New Orleans, the British passed Cuba and headed for the Florida coast. There they lay at the entrance to Pensacola Bay for nearly 48 hours, wind-bound by a westerly gale.

Early on the morning of December 2, 1814, Jackson and his escort reached Fort St. John at the point where Bayou St. John empties into Lake Pontchartrain. This was the back door to New Orleans, which was only six miles away. Jackson dispatched a courier with a letter to Bernard de Marigny de Mandeville within the city. The courier met Marigny at the corner of Chartres and St. Louis Streets and gave him the letter. Marigny opened it and found it was from his father-in-law, Don Juan Ventura Morales, Governor of the Floridas.

Don Juan had been the Spanish Intendent at New Orleans before Louisiana was transferred to the United States, and had continued to act as Intendent (making concession and sales of land in territory in dispute between the United States and Spain) until 1806, when he went to Pensacola.[9] When Jackson took that city, Morales insisted on being his host and as Jackson left, gave him the letter for his son-in-law.

After Marigny had read it, the courier asked if it would be agreeable for General Jackson to establish headquarters at his home the next day. Marigny replied that he "would receive with great pleasure the Conqueror of the Floridas, and of Colonel Nicholls, who had maltreated his old compatriots in Pensacola and had carried away a great number of their slaves." Then he sent the courier back to Jackson with the message that he would receive General Jackson the next day and that breakfast would be awaiting him.[10]

Meanwhile, Jackson and his escort rode up the muddy road along the bank of Bayou St. John until they came to a villa near the junction of Canal Carondelet which connected the bayou with the

---

[9] *Ibid.*, 70-73, 113.
[10] Marigny, *Reflection on the Campaign*, 20.

city. The villa was the suburban retreat of J. Kilty Smith, a rich merchant. Here the horsemen dismounted and had breakfast.

After breakfast Mr. Smith supplied a carriage in which Jackson rode into the city. Governor Claiborne, Mayor Nicholas Girod (" a rotund, affable, pleasant old French gentleman, of easy, polite manners "), the citizens' defense committee, and the legislature's defense committee hastened to meet him. They led him to a three-story building at 106 Royal Street.

Soon Royal Street was filled with people and Jackson appeared on the second story gallery to speak to them. Livingston was by his side and translated Jackson's words into French. Marigny was with the crowd below. He heard the General say: " I have come to protect the city. I will drive our enemies into the sea or perish in the effort. Good citizens, you must all rally around me in this emergency, cease all differences and divisions, and unite with me in patriotic resolve to save this city from dishonor and disaster which a presumptuous enemy threatens to inflict upon it." [11]

Bernard de Marigny de Mandeville, with that clarity and logic peculiar to Frenchmen, was able to put into words how the citizens of New Orleans felt when they heard and saw Andrew Jackson. They all had wanted to fight but there had been " a sense of uneasiness arising from a defect of organization. Governor Claiborne was a very honest man of personal bravery, but he had not the energy necessary to give a great impulse to the population of Louisiana." Here was a man who could.[12]

Edward Livingston, his brother-in-law August de Castera Davezac, and John Randolph Grymes, members of the *citizens'* defense committee, immediately attached themselves to Jackson and became part of his staff. They spoke French and neither Jackson nor any of his regular adjutants understood the language.

Bernard de Marigny did not try to become one of Jackson's aides-de-camp. His pride was hurt when the General decided to make

[11] Walker, *Jackson and New Orleans*, 14; Parton, *Life of Jackson*, II, 29.
[12] Marigny, *Reflection on the Campaign*, 2; Gayarré, *History of Louisiana*, IV, 398.

106 Royal Street his headquarters. So Marigny, chairman of the *legislative* defense committee, joined Claiborne's staff.

Jackson immediately wanted to know the military strength of the city. He reviewed the Battalion d'Orleáns with its five companies of militia—287 men. Their captains, four Frenchmen and one Irishman, were all naturalized citizens. Captain J. B. Plauché, a Creole of Louisiana, commanded the Carabiniers d'Orleáns, the best-equipped and best-trained company. Little five-foot Baron Henri de Saint-Gème, with a foot-high plume in his cap, put his Dragons à Pied through their paces. St. Gème was an emigrant from Haiti, and Dominique You's partner.

Captain Jean Hudri of the Francs and Captain Auguste Guibert of the Chasseurs were the other Creole commanders. The Irish captain, Maunsel White, was the "Ajax of the army. In spite of his tall stature, increased by a high plume, he never bowed his head to bullets nor Congreve." [13] His corps was made up entirely of Irishmen.

These were the available white troops. The population of New Orleans, as given by different authorities, varied between 18,000 and 20,000 at this time. The sources agree that 5,000 of these were slaves. Subtracting these and women, children, old and infirm, and the sick, meant that about 2,000 men (white and free people of color) were available for militia or regular troops. Marigny says that, of these 2,000, not more than 300 were Anglo-Saxons. [14]

The New Orleans Militia, the City Rifles which were soon to be organized, and the 7th and 44th Regiments totaled approximately 1,200. [15] The difference of 800 represented the free people of color who, due to Claiborne's dilatory tactics, had not been organized as a battalion. [16]

Jackson had confidence in the militia troops and told them so; but he did not let them see his concern because there were no guns

---

[13] Marigny, *Reflection on the Campaign*, 12.
[14] *Ibid.*, 17.
[15] *Ibid.*; Adams, *History of United States*, VIII, 334.
[16] Bassett, *Life of Andrew Jackson*, 156-57.

for his army except 500 old muskets and 7,500 flint pistols obtained from the Baratarians. He did have two mortars. They had been landed from bomb-ketches which had been condemned. But there were not 100 bombs of the caliber required for these mortars.[17]

Meanwhile, all the engineers of New Orleans were called together so that Jackson could consult with them about topography and defense. Then Jackson sent detachments " to fell timbers against every small bayou and creek through which a passage for boats and barges could be afforded; and to increase the obstruction, by sinking large frames in their beds, and filling them with earth." [18]

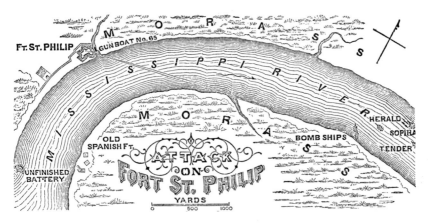

Commodore Patterson had by this time stationed on Lake Borgne his old gig, the *Alligator,* and the five gunboats that had been used against the Baratarians. Trusting in these " eyes and ears " to give warning of any enemy approach, Jackson with Patterson, Livingston and other aides, and two engineers sailed down the Mississippi on an inspection tour.

Because of the nature of the river, no defense was attempted below Fort St. Philip, fifty miles from the mouth. Jackson gave instructions for strengthening this fort and then came back up the river. He

---

[17] Bassett (ed.), *Correspondence,* II, 110; Adams, *History of United States,* VIII, 334; Gayarré, *History of Louisiana,* IV, 385.
[18] John Henry Eaton, *The Life of Andrew Jackson* (Philadelphia, 1824), 274.

stopped at English Turn and ordered batteries of heavy cannon placed so as to destroy any armed vessel that might try to pass. No vessel could round the Turn without waiting for a proper wind. During the wait a few guns could destroy any enemy ship.

Jackson and Patterson were back in New Orleans by December 9. A friendly Choctaw handed Patterson a letter. It was in French and unsigned. The Choctaw said the man who sent it was " dark-complexioned, had a long mustache, and spoke like a Frenchman." [19] The letter was dated Pensacola, December 5, 1815, and said:

Sir

    I feel it a duty to apprize you of a very large force of the enemy off this port, and it is generally understood New Orleans is the object of attack. It amounts at present to about eighty vessels, and more than double that number are momentarily looked for, to form a junction, when an immediate commencement of their operations will take place. I am not able to learn how, when, or where the attack will be made; but I heard that they have vessels of all descriptions, and a large body of troops. Admiral Cochrane commands, and his ship, the Tonnant, lies at this moment just outside the bar; and probably no means will be left untried to obtain their object. The admiral arrived only yesterday noon.[20]

Patterson took the letter to Jackson. He considered it trustworthy, so Patterson sent these instructions to Tac (Thomas Ap Catesby) Jones, lieutenant in command of the gunboat flotilla on Lake Borgne: " Proceed to Pass Christian for reconnaissance. If the enemy force tries to cut off the gunboats, retreat to the Rigolets. There with the protection and help of Fort Petites Coquilles, sink the enemy or be sunk." [21]

Then Jackson visited the area back of the city. He rode along Bayou Sauvage or Gentilly to its confluence with Chef Menteur— one mile from where Chef Menteur disembogues into Lake Borgne and Lake Pontchartrain in such a way that it forms a pass between the two lakes. Jackson ordered a fort to be built at the point where Bayou Sauvage joins Chef Menteur. This would command the

---

[19] Buell, *History of Jackson*, I, 370.
[20] Latour, *Historical Memoir*, Appendix No. XVIII, xxxii.
[21] *Ibid.*, 57-58.

Gentilly plain which was high ground and gave easy access to the city. A few miles to the east was another pass between the two lakes, Pass Rigolets, and its unfinished fort, Petites Coquilles.

By this time Jackson knew the worst. He had approximately 500 militia, two infantry regiments, Fort St. Philip on the Mississippi, a sloop of war and a schooner on that river, Fort Petites Coquilles on the Rigolets, five gunboats and the *Alligator* on Lake Borgne, Fort St. John on Lake Pontchartrain back of the city, and a very small supply of arms and ammunition with which to defend New Orleans and the 600 miles of Louisiana coast.

THE BRITISH CAMP BELOW

NEW ORLEANS

While Jackson thought all his orders were being executed, Admiral Cochrane's invasion fleet approached Chandeleur Island. On December 8, his 74's anchored off that island while the rest of the fleet took a position between Ship and Cat Island.[1] Only the lighter vessels could navigate from this point which was the entrance to Mississippi Sound—the shoal coastal waters between Mobile and Lake Borgne.

Cochrane had a good understanding of the area, not only from maps and books published a few years earlier by English observers in America but also from information which certain Spaniards, formerly residents of New Orleans, gave him. This was confirmed by Spanish fishermen who had a village of 20 or 30 huts about one mile from the mouth of Bayou Bienvenu which emptied into Lake Borgne.

The British could not attack New Orleans from the mouth of the Mississippi. Vessels dependent upon sails could not hope to pass Fort St. Philip and English Turn against the strong current of the river. Neither could they enter Lake Pontchartrain and attack New

---

[1] There are two Cat Islands along the coast: this one in the Mississippi Sound and the other in the large bay west of Bayou Lafourche delta where Laffite operated. The bay west of Lafourche is called Cat Island Lake.

Orleans from the rear because Cochrane thought Fort Petites Coquilles defending the entrance to Lake Pontchartrain had 40 pieces
of artillery mounted and 500 troops. These would be sufficient to
annihilate any force that tried to enter the lake through the Rigolets.[2]

Cochrane decided to bypass the Rigolets and attack New Orleans
from a point which he could reach by crossing Lake Borgne and
ascending Bayou Bienvenu. The mouth of this bayou was 60 miles
from where his ships were anchored. His plan was to land all the
troops on Isle-aux-Pois which was midway between the ships and
the mouth of the bayou. He had only enough small vessels to
transport one-third of his troops at a time. From Isle-aux-Pois the
landing craft, guided by Spanish fishermen, could transport troops
in relays the 30 remaining miles to Bayou Bienvenu.[3]

Meanwhile, Tac Jones and his five gunboats had been studying the
concentration of British ships between Ship and Cat Island.[4] The
British sighted the gunboats on December 12. They would have to
be captured because Cochrane's troops had to be ferried 60 miles
in open boats. Jones saw that the British had discovered him and
scurried before the wind, hoping to make the 50 miles to Fort
Petites Coquilles on the Rigolets.

In hot pursuit was Captain Lockyer (the same Captain Lockyer
who had been sent to Jean Laffite) with 45 barges, 43 cannon and
1,200 sailors and marines. This flotilla pursued the gunboats two
days.[5]

---

[2] William James, *A Full and Correct Account of the Military Occurrences of the
Late War Between Great Britain and the United States of America* (2 vols., London,
1818), II, 358; Mahan, *Sea Power and the War of 1812*, II, 388.

[3] Mahan, *Sea Power and the War of 1812*, 388-89.

[4] Jones had stationed his gunboats and the *Alligator* at Bay St. Louis where there were
public stores and a schooner, the *Seahorse*, sailing master William Johnson, commander.
On the morning of December 13, Jones sent the *Seahorse* into Bay St. Louis to bring
away public stores from the position he had evacuated. Johnson, finding it impossible
to escape, blew up the schooner, set fire to the stores on shore, and escaped with his
crew by land. Latour, *Historical Memoir*, Appendix No. XIX, xxxii-xxxvi; Robert B.
M'Afee, *History of the Late War* (Lexington, 1816), 505-506.

[5] Tac Jones's letter to Benjamin W. Crowinshield, Secretary of the Navy, March 12,
1815, reporting the battle, is quoted in various sources: William James, *Military Occurrences*, II, 526-28; *Niles' Register*, VIII (April 22, 1815), 126, 345; Latour, *Historical*

On the morning of December 14, Jones and the gunboats had bad luck. The wind died away completely at 1 A. M. The gunboats were between Malheureux Island and Point Claire on the mainland. Jones stationed the gunboats in line across the channel and waited.

About 9:30 Captain Lockyer saw Commodore Porter's old gig, the *Alligator*, trying to join the five gunboats. He detached four boats with nearly 200 men to capture this cockle-shell. In his report he described his splendid prize as " an armed sloop." [6]

One hour later the enemy came within range and the gunboats deliberately opened fire. The battle lasted three hours. Ten Americans were killed and 35 wounded. All the gunboat captains except one were wounded. The British captured the gunboats at a cost of 17 men killed and 77 wounded.[7] They returned to Cat Island with their prisoners and captured gunboats.

Jones and the other wounded were put on the *Gorgon*, a large storeship. There a tall and gentlemanly individual conversed freely with them " respecting his future arrangements for the discharge of his duty." He was to be the future " collector of the revenue of his Britannic Majesty in the Port of New Orleans." [8]

Memoir, Appendix No. XIX, xxxiii-xxxv; John Henry Eaton, *The Life of Andrew Jackson* (Philadelphia, 1824), 275-81.

[6] Nicholas Lockyer to Admiral Cochrane, December 17, 1814, quoted in Latour, *Historical Memoir*, Appendix No. LXVI, cxl. This " armed sloop " mounted one 4-pounder and carried eight men.

The English navy has been greatly overrated, perhaps, because it dominated European seas where it had little competition. One English captain, during service in America at this time, wrote: " I was placed as a supernumerary on the books of the *Magnificent*, and very shortly after received my commission as commander of a ten-gun brig. These vessels are so admirably constructed as neither to be able to fight or fly, as occasion may require. They are the most useless class of vessels ever constructed, and are admirably calculated to depress the courage of our seamen, and to heighten that of our adversaries. There is not a ten-gun brig in the service which is a match for any smart American schooner with a long gun on board. . . . The same remarks are applicable to the little, short, useless, leewardly class of ships called Jack-ass frigates, out of compliment to the proposer or builder, I know not which, of these deformed vessels. An American sloop of war ought to take them with a certainty." Frederick Chamier, *The Life of a Sailor* (2 vols., New York, 1833), II, 127.

[7] Report of Captain Lockyer, quoted in Adams, *History of United States*, VIII, 336; Eaton, *Life of Jackson*, 281; Latour, *Historical Memoir*, Appendix No. LXVI, cxlii-cxliii.

[8] Walker, *Jackson and New Orleans*, 109-10.

As soon as Patterson heard about the gunboat battle, he sent two men under a flag of truce to the British fleet. They were Thomas Shields, purser of the New Orleans naval station, and Dr. Robert Morrell. Shields was to try to get the prisoners released on parole and Morrell was to attend the wounded. Admiral Cochrane thought the real purpose of these two was to get information. He questioned them without learning anything important. However, observing that Shields was deaf, Cochrane had Shields and the doctor placed in a room where their conversation could be overheard.

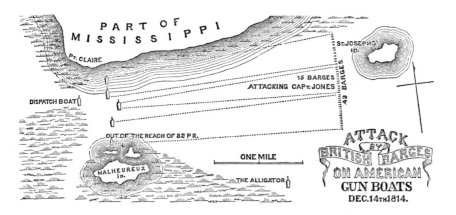

The two suspected this purpose. After everyone had retired and all was quiet, they began to speak in loud voices of why they had been detained and how they had not given any vital information. "How greatly these gentlemen will be disappointed in their expectations," said Shields, "for Jackson with the twenty thousand troops he now has, and the reinforcements from Kentucky which must speedily reach him, will be able to destroy any force that can be landed from these ships." [9]

Major General John Keane, who was in temporary command of the British army, and Admiral Cochrane pondered this information.

[9] Eaton, *Life of Jackson*, 287-88.

The next day Shields and Morrell were sent to the *Gorgon*, and they were not released until January 12, 1815.[10]

One British officer who had witnessed the gunboat battle said, " I have always regarded this affair as a wanton sacrifice of human life, merely to maintain the idle boast of bull dog pertinacity." [11] However, the victory was necessary. It gave the British command of Lake Borgne, which meant that during the next nine days they landed troops and made their beachhead without being discovered or disturbed.

While troops were assembling on Isle-aux-Pois, Admiral Cochrane sent an embassy to the Choctaws whose allegiance had wavered after Jackson drove the British from Pensacola. Gleig went along and found the expedition amusing. The Englishmen had to stay overnight with the Choctaws for they would not be hurried. Then, having presented the warriors with muskets and ammunition, the British departed, taking with them the two chiefs at their own request. " For this journey they had equipped themselves in a most extraordinary manner; making their appearance in scarlet jackets, which they had obtained from Colonel Nickolls, old-fashioned steel-bound cocked hats, and shoes. Trowsers they would not wear, but permitted their lower parts to remain with no other covering than a girdle tied round their loins; and sticking scalping knives in their belts, and holding tomahawks in their hands, they accompanied us to the fleet, and took up their residence with the Admiral." [12]

These chiefs joined others already on the flagship. Captain Benson Earle Hill says that on its quarter-deck he saw, " for the first time the Indian chiefs, who we were led to believe, would prove valuable allies to us in the present undertaking. A British officer, Colonel Nicholls of the Marines, had for some time past been domesticated with them; from his account of their prowess, and attachment to our cause, most favourable results were anticipated." [13]

---

[10] Latour, *Historical Memoir*, 75-77.
[11] Chesterton, *Peace, War and Adventure*, I, 179.
[12] Gleig, *Narrative of Campaigns*, 1821 London edition, 264-70.
[13] *Recollections of an Artillery Officer*, I, 299.

George Laval Chesterton, another officer, was shocked when he saw his friend Colonel Nicholls look " so strangely care-worn." And when Nicholls urged him to help him with his Indians, Chesterton " adroitly referred Nicholls to Colonel Dickson " and privately expressed to that colonel his " earnest desire to be spared the horrors of so questionable a service." Dickson thereupon told Nicholls that he could not spare Chesterton and hence for Chesterton " all danger of marauding and scalping was obviated." [14]

In the meantime, Cochrane had sent two officers in a boat to reconnoiter the area below New Orleans via Bayou Bienvenu. They were disguised as fishermen and some of the Spanish fishermen were their guides. They reached the bayou and ascended to the village of the fishermen.

Why had this bayou not been obstructed? Jackson had given particular orders with regard to Bayou Bienvenu. This important assignment had been committed, " in the first instance, to a detachment from the 7th Regt.—afterwards to Col. de Laronde of the Louisiana militia, and lastly, to make all sure, to Majr. Genl. Villeré commanding the district between the river and the lakes, and who being a native of the country, was presumed to be best acquainted with all those passes." [15]

Perhaps the fishermen had something to do with the situation. They were accustomed to fish in Lake Borgne and then to take their fish in pirogues to the canals of De Laronde's and Villeré's plantations and thence by wagons up the River Road to New Orleans.

At the village the two Englishmen got into a pirogue and with their guides ascended Bayou Bienvenu to its main branch, Bayou Manzant, and up that branch to the canal which drained Villeré's plantation. At its head the Englishmen jumped out and walked to the Mississippi—1,000 yards away.

They were nine miles below New Orleans. The road along the

---

[14] *Peace, War and Adventure*, I, 213-14.
[15] Jackson to Secretary of War Monroe, Camp below New Orleans, December 27, 1814, Bassett (ed.), *Correspondence*, II, 126-27.

levee and the firm strip of plantation land next to the river would make a good spout through which to funnel the invasion army into the city. The officers decided that the best place for the British to establish their encampment would be on Villeré's plantation, Lacoste's plantation, and De Laronde's plantation.

DE LA RONDE'S MANSION.

They questioned the fishermen, saying, " How many men does General Jackson have in New Orleans? "

" Not many," was the answer, " not more than two thousand."

All the fishermen except one went with the officers back to Isle-aux-Pois. The one left behind was sick.

By December 21, all the British troops had been landed on Isle-aux-Pois. No women were taken to the island. They remained on the larger ships. The women of Captain Crawford's company were left on the *Anne*, a transport.[16] While Major General Keane reviewed his troops on Isle-aux-Pois, Major Gabriel Villeré sent a picket of eight men and a sergeant to the fishermen's village.

---

[16] Chesterton, *Peace, War and Adventure*, I, 203.

"All the others are out in the lake fishing," the sick fisherman told them. The sergeant in command did not question this statement. He posted a sentinel, sent a man at intervals two or three miles into the lake, and learned nothing.

Meanwhile, along the beach of Isle-aux-Pois boats from every ship in the fleet were assembling to move the troops. A subaltern gives us a vivid description of the procedure. He records that " to protect the rear against annoyance, each launch, as well as some of the barges, was armed with a twelve-pound carronade in the bows; whilst the six cutters lately captured from the enemy, with all the tenders and small craft brought from the Chesapeake, prepared to accompany them. After everything, even to the captain's gigs, had been put in requisition, it appeared that hardly one-third of the army could move at a time; but even thus our leaders determined upon entering immediately upon the business." [17]

The 22nd of December dawned cold and rainy. At nine o'clock in the morning

the advance of the army, under the command of Colonel Thornton, stepped into the boats. It consisted in all of about fifteen hundred infantry, two pieces of light cannon, and a troop of rockets, and it was accompanied by General Keane in person, the heads of the engineer and commissariat departments, a competent number of medical officers, and the Indian chiefs. . . .

The boat in which Charlton and myself were embarked was a man-of-war's barge, rowed by six oars of a side, and commanded by a midshipman. Besides the seamen, there was crowded into it not fewer than sixty men and four officers, so that the full complement amounted to seventy-eight souls. Under these circumstances the space granted to each individual was not very commodious. It was by no means an easy task to shift our postures after they had once been assumed, for we were as completely wedged together as were ever a child's bricks in their box, or a bundle of logs in what is called a cord of wood. As long, however, as it continued dry overhead, the inconvenience thence arising was little felt; but we had not proceeded more than a mile from the place of embarkation, when the black clouds suddenly opened, and the rain fell as if a thousand shower-baths had been all at once opened upon us. Then our situation became comfortless

---

[17] *A Subaltern in America,* 1833 Philadelphia edition, 206.

enough. In the difficulty of adjusting ourselves at all, cloaks and greatcoats necessarily lost their clasps, and the neck and shoulders were left bare. Water ran down our backs and shoulders like the sewers in Ludgate Hill after a thunder-storm, yet was there much in the appearance of all about us calculated to carry our thoughts beyond the present moment,—at all events, to make us think lightly of present grievances. Not fewer than an hundred boats, of all shapes and sizes, were making way in regular column over the surface of the lake; they were all filled, to repletion, with armed men, and not a sound issued from them, except that which the rowing occasioned, and an occasional word of command uttered by those in authority. The boats moved in lines of ten a-breast; a little way a-head of them sailed a couple of cutters; the like number protected each of the flanks; and the rear was covered by three traders. . . . Sir Alexander Cochrane, in a light schooner, kept just so far apart as to see at a glance how things were going, and to superintend the whole. . . .

But the prospect of passing the night cramped and cooped up as we were, was certainly not hailed by any one with either satisfaction or indifference. The rain had fallen in such quantities, as not only to saturate the clothing of every individual, but seriously to incommode us, by creating a pool ankle-deep in the bottom of the boat, while, on account of our crowded state, we could not succeed in baling it. It ceased, however, at last, and was succeeded by a keen frost, and a northerly wind as sharp and cutting as any mortal would desire to face. . . .

As day dawned, a singularly wild and uninviting waste of country opened out before us. We were now within a stone's throw of the American shore, and ran along its edge in search of the mouth of the creek. It was a complete bog. A bank of black earth, or rather black mud, covered with tall reeds, constituted the single feature of the landscape. Not a trace of human industry, not a tree or bush of any kind or description, not even a mound or hillock, served to break in upon the sameness of scene. One wide waste of reeds alone met the eye, except at the very edge of the water, where the slime which nourished them lay slightly exposed. . . .

At length the mouth of a creek or inlet, wide at first, but rapidly narrowing, presented itself. Towards it the Admiral immediately directed his course; but the schooner in which he was embarked drew too much water, and in a few minutes went aground. We could not make any effort to relieve him from his awkward situation, for this was not a moment at which serious delay could be tolerated, and our boats were all too heavily laden already, to admit of their taking additional passengers on board. Onwards, therefore, we swept, the banks on either hand closing in upon us more and more as we proceeded, till first we were necessitated to contract our front, from five boats a-breast to three, and finally only one. We were now steering up a narrow cut, which measured at its widest spot, not more than twenty feet across, and which, in some parts, became so exceedingly narrow, that the rowers ceased to dip the oars in the water, and propelled us by punting alone. Yet it was an admirable spot for the conduct of a secret expedition. As far as we could judge from the appearance of the soil, the bogs on either hand seemed quite impassable even for infantry. It was covered by reeds, so lofty as to obscure any object which could float in the canal. No eye could therefore watch our proceedings; and though we, too, were shut out from beholding all other objects besides our own line of boats and the blue sky, there was not a man amongst us who entertained the slightest apprehension that danger could be near.[18]

In the small hours of the morning of December 23, a sentinel at the fishermen's village heard something. He aroused the picket. They saw five barges full of men ascending the bayou.

The Americans hid behind the cabins until the barges passed. Then they silently entered a small boat and rowed for the lake. Occupants in one of the English barges looked back. They saw the escaping Americans, chased after the little boat, and captured it. One man contrived to escape. He floundered in the swamps for two days before he found his way to Jackson's army.

The captured men were shut up in a cabin. An officer came in, looked them over and pointed to Joe Ducros. The redcoats put Joe in a small boat and took him to Major General Keane for questioning.

"How many men has General Jackson in New Orleans?" Keane asked.

"Maybe twelve, maybe fifteen thousand. He has about four thousand at English Turn," Joe answered.[19]

Keane was disturbed. Jackson must have 20,000 troops. That doctor and purser sent by Commodore Patterson under a flag of truce had said so, and now Ducros said the same thing. They could not possibly have talked with Ducros.

Meanwhile, Colonel Thornton advanced to the edge of Villeré

---

[18] *Ibid.*, 207-12.
[19] Walker, *Jackson and New Orleans*, 123-24.

VILLERÉ'S MANSION.

plantation. Under cover of an orange grove, he and his men approached the "Big House," Major Gabriel Villeré was sitting on the gallery facing the Mississippi, watching his brother Célestin clean a gun. He looked up and saw the redcoats and almost immediately the two brothers were made prisoners.

Major General Keane arrived and decided to halt. Thornton pleaded with him to move on. He pointed out that the fishermen were right about Jackson's strength—2,000 troops—and that in two hours they could be in New Orleans. The troops were fresh, in excellent spirits, and full of confidence.

Major General Keane would not be persuaded. If the fishermen were wrong and Jackson did have 20,000 troops, the British might be attacked and cut off by overwhelming numbers before reinforcements could reach them. "We can afford to wait," he told Thornton. "In twelve hours two thousand more troops will be here and soon after that the rest of the army. Place your men next the levee. We will bivouac here tonight and attack in the morning."

Thornton was shocked, but he put his troops in postition one hundred yards from the river and sent men to post handbills on buildings and fences. These had been printed in French and Spanish on the invasion press. They said:

Louisianians! Remain quiet in your houses. Your slaves shall be preserved to you, and your property respected. We make war only against Americans.

Admiral Cochrane
Major General Keane [20]

Several parties were sent in all direction to reconnoitre. They returned with an account that no enemy, nor any traces of an enemy, could be discerned.

The troops were accordingly suffered to light fires, and make themselves comfortable; only their accoutrements were not taken off, and the arms were piled in such form as to be within reach at a moment's notice.

As soon as these agreeable orders were issued, the soldiers proceeded to obey them both in letter and in spirit. Tearing up a number of strong palings, large fires were lighted in a moment; water was brought from the river, and provisions were cooked. But their bare rations did not content them. Spreading themselves over the country as far as a regard to safety would permit, they entered every house, and brought away quantities of hams, fowls, and wines of various descriptions; which being divided among them, all fared well, and none received too large a quantity. In this division of good things, they were not unmindful of their officers; for upon active warfare the officers are considered by the privates as comrades, to whom respect and obedience are due, rather than as masters.

It was now about three o'clock in the afternoon, and all had as yet remained quiet. The troops having finished their meal, lay stretched besides their fires, or refreshed themselves by bathing, for to-day the heat was such as to render this latter employment extremely agreeable, when suddenly a bugle from the advanced posts sounded the alarm, which was echoed back from all in the army. Starting up, we stood to our arms, and prepared for battle, the alarm being now succeeded by some firing; but we were scarcely in order, when word was sent from the front that there was no danger, only a few horse having made their appearance, who were checked and put to flight at the first discharge. Upon this intelligence, our wonted confidence returned, and we again betook ourselves to our

---

[20] Latour, *Historical Memoir*, 91.

former occupations, remarking that, as the American had never yet dared to attack, there was no great probability of their doing so on the present occasion.[21]

[21] Gleig, *Narrative of Campaigns*, 1821, London edition, 282-83.
". . . the English army dominated the whole extent of territory from Chalmette plantation to Terre-au Boeufs and in following Terre-au-Boeufs to Lake Borgne. Consequently all inhabitants below Chalmette plantation were prisoners of the English, who had the right to seize all the provisions of the inhabitants as well as the power to force them to bring it to the camps in their carts. But, instead of seizing the provisions and animals without paying for them, they paid for them more than they were really worth originally. In a word, they did what the American army did in New Mexico on its march to Vera Cruz and until their moment of embarkation to return to the United States." Marigny, *Reflections on the Campaign*, 8.

"THEY SHALL NOT REST

ON OUR SOIL!"

NEWS OF THE CAPTURE OF THE GUNBOATS ARRIVED IN NEW Orleans on the afternoon of December 15. Jackson was not in the city, he was on his way there from Chef Menteur. Rumors spread by the enemy caused the city to panic. When Jackson arrived he issued a General Order which looked the danger square in the face and convinced the citizens that this man could and would command the situation.

Then Jackson called out the Louisiana State Militia. Major General Jacques Villeré—he whose plantation the British were approaching—was in command of the first division. He had already rallied men in the outlying areas and soon " from all the parishes the inhabitants could be seen coming with their hunting guns for in the city there were not enough guns in the magazines of the United States to arm the citizens." [1]

Major Pierre Lacoste—whose plantation was next to Villeré's—had already organized and drilled a battalion of free men of color. These were sent with two pieces of cannon down the Gentilly road to erect a battery at the confluence of Bayou Sauvage and Chef Menteur. So pleased was Jackson with this battalion that he had ordered another organized. Savary, a colored man from Haiti who

---

[1] Marigny, *Reflection on the Campaign*, 3.

had served as an officer under the French Republic and who was known as a man of great courage, organized this second battalion and then in accordance with Jackson's policy handed it over to a white man, Major Louis Daquin.[2]

Feliciana dragoons hurried after Lacoste and his battalion to help cover the Gentilly plain. They had been quartered in the upper suburb of the city for some time and had already reconnoitered passes toward Chef Menteur and settlements below Villeré's plantation at Terre-aux-Boeufs.[3]

Pierre Jugeat was sent to organize a company of friendly Choctaws. Jugeat was the son of a Creole French trader by a half-breed Choctaw woman whose white blood was also French. He had received some education at a Catholic academy in New Orleans but he had also lived among the Indians. He was " a man of unusual intelligence, fine personal appearance and a thorough gentleman in deportment. Living among the Indians, speaking all their dialects and well acquainted with their leading men, he was invaluable to Jackson as a scout during the Creek War." [4]

Jackson had not concentrated his forces, he dared not, until he knew where the British would strike. He was certain of the approximate target by the day the gunboat battle was fought, for on that date he ordered Brigadier General John Coffee in the neighborhood of Baton Rouge to come immediately to New Orleans.

Coffee was in camp at the mouth of Sandy Creek which flows into the Amite. His men had been foraging without much success because he did not have cash with which to buy at a low price. Jackson's orders reached him at 8 P. M., December 16. At four the next morning he was writing Jackson saying: " Shall move my command this morning at sunrise. . . . I think we will reach you in four days, say by the evening of the 20th instant. . . . My arms are in bad condition . . . we have from 2 to 4 hundred that are not good . . . all my powder was destroyed by the rains." [5]

---

[2] *Ibid.*, 12; Gayarré, *History of Louisiana*, IV, 406; Latour, *Historical Memoir*, 64.
[3] Bassett (ed.), *Correspondence*, II, 84, 91.
[4] Buell, *History of Jackson*, I, 245.
[5] Bassett (ed.), *Correspondence*, II, 117.

The matter of arms and ammunition was getting more and more critical. During the summer Jackson had written the Secretary of War asking that such be sent to New Orleans. They should have arrived in October. It was not until November that part of a supply was sent from Pittsburgh. When Major General Carroll and his Tennesseans arrived at Natchez at 10 P. M., December 13, there was a keelboat behind him " freighted with about 14.00 stand of Arms and ammunition for the use of the Army." These were the Pittsburgh supplies. William Carroll sent a messenger to Jackson saying, ". . . a great number of my Men being badly armed, and many others not armed at all, I wish to ascertain if you will not permit me to furnish them from this boat." [6]

Meanwhile, Major General John Thomas was on his way with Kentucky Militia. Kentucky was not within Jackson's military district, but the governor of Kentucky had cooperated with his request and had mustered into service 2,300 men and officers, who, under the command of Thomas, were at the mouth of the Cumberland River on December 8. Thomas wrote Jackson that it would take 20 or 25 days to get as far as Natchez. [7]

While militia from Kentucky and Tennessee, Hinds's Mississippi Dragoons, and Coffee's brigades were on their way, Jackson was not idle. Before the gunboat battle Patterson had complained that he did not have enough seamen, so Jackson had asked the legislature to suspend the writ of habeas corpus in order that seamen might be impressed. Louis Louaillier was chairman of the committee to which this request was referred. The committee decided that men forced into the service would not be good defenders of the country. This may have been the beginning of that antagonism between Jackson and Louaillier that would have repercussions later.

Jackson requested a second time that the writ of habeas corpus be suspended. Not only did the legislature refuse this request but it also refused to adjourn because conditions might arise when the intervention of the legislature might be necessary. Apparently, the

---

[6] *Ibid.*, 113.
[7] *Ibid.*, 115.

legislature did not believe that Jackson could solve Louisiana's defense problem. Jackson did not quibble with it. On December 16, he proclaimed strict martial law. Notices were posted containing the rules that would be rigidly enforced.

Not a voice was raised in protest and so great was the confidence in Jackson that not a shop, not a warehouse was closed, nor any valuables removed from the city.[8] Private hospitals were established and the women formed committees to provide all that was necessary. Citizens contributed lint, clothing and bed linen. The old men under Gaspard De Bruys organized themselves to protect the city.[9] A company of volunteer riflemen was formed "under the command of a Mr. Beale, a man of advanced years, a native of Virginia. . . . This company was principally made up of Americans from the northern states, and people of some instruction: it numbered among its ranks Mr. B. Lewis, Judge of the District Court in Louisiana, B. Chew, Director of the Custom House, Messrs. Montgomery & Touro, wealthy and respectable merchants, the merchants Story, Kenner, and Henderson, the lawyer Pouter de Peyster, and many others."[10]

All able-bodied men except Englishmen were pressed into service.

Even the legislature fell into line. It adopted measures designed to aid citizens who had " to leave their private affairs in a state of abandonment, which might expose them to great distress." It passed an act to grant delays which provided that no notes or bills of exchange could be legally collected for 120 days, that no property should be sold during the same space of time, and that no civil suit or action should be commenced and that all pending suits should cease until the first of May, 1815.[11]

On one point, all the citizens disagreed with their general—they could not understand why he would have nothing to do with the Baratarians. They set to work to get that stubborn soul to relent,

---

[8] Latour, *Historical Memoir*, 73.
[9] Marigny, *Reflection on the Campaign*, 3.
[10] Nolte, *Fifty Years in Both Hemispheres*, 206.
[11] Gayarré, *History of Louisiana*, IV, 412-13.

" to remove the antipathy he had conceived against the Baratarians." Major Villeré was their first spokesman. He pointed out that Patterson had no sailors to man the *Louisiana* and the *Carolina*, and that Jackson had very few artillerymen. If he would only say the word, he would have the best sailors in the world and the most skillful gunners. But Jackson would not say the word and Villeré left him feeling that he had failed. However, Jackson's frontier instinct was telling him that he had misjudged the Baratarians, that it would be folly to persist in his mistaken notion.

So the next day when Bernard de Marigny and his defense committee broached the subject, Jackson replied, " The Baratarians are now being prosecuted by civil officers of the United States. Many are in prison and I cannot do anything in the matter." [12]

Taking the hint, the committee went to Judge Dominick Augustus Hall and told him what Jackson had said. " I am general in these circumstances," replied Judge Hall. " Present at once a resolution in the legislature demanding that the procedures against these men be suspended for four months and I will immediately give my orders to the District Attorney of the United States." [13]

This resolution was presented the next day and passed unanimously. Prosecution ceased and Judge Hall immediately released Dominique You and the rest of the Baratarians who were in the Cabildo.

Baratarians and their leaders appeared from everywhere. Patterson soon had splendid crews on his two ships. Dominique and Jean Laffite hastened to Jackson. They ran into him on the corner of St. Philip and Royal Street.[14]

Jean Laffite assured Jackson that he could supply cannon and all the ammunition that his army needed. At headquarters Laffite placed his maps and knowledge at the general's service, and sent his agents to deliver the war matériel. Dominique and Beluche set to work organizing three companies of artillery.

---

[12] Marigny, *Reflection on the Campaign*, 3.
[13] *Ibid.*, 4.
[14] *Journal of Jean Laffite*, 58.

Jackson held a review of the city militia and the newly organized company of men of color on December 18. Then he sent Plauché with his five companies of the Battalion d'Orléans to Fort St. John on Lake Pontchartrain behind the city. Both Dominique You and Beluche and one company of artillery went with Plauché. The other two companies of Baratarian artillery were sent elsewhere—one to Fort Petites Coquilles and the other to Fort St. Philip.

The work of obstructing bayous west of the Mississippi was under the command of Major Michael Reynolds. His headquarters were at The Temple, in the very heart of the area where Laffite had munition depots. Jackson's powder magazine was on the west side of the Mississippi, at a point a short distance below New Orleans. Nothing must happen to interrupt or destroy the delivery of powder to Jackson's magazine. Jean Laffite knew the network of vital communications better than any one else. Jackson sent him to Reynolds with this letter: "Mr. Jean Laffite has offered me his services to go down and give you every information in his power. You will therefore please to afford him the necessary protection from Injury and Insult and when you have derived the information you wish furnish him with your passport for his return dismissing him as soon as possible as I shall want him here." [15]

Coffee and his men came in on the 20th. He had commenced his march with 1,250 men, having left behind at Sandy Creek 300 who were on the sick list. The weather was cold and rainy, the terrain difficult, but 50 miles were covered the first day. The terrific pace slowed down 500 of his mounted. Coffee gave orders that all who were able were to advance with him, the rest to follow as fast as their exhausted horses permitted. Coffee and 800 men rode 70 miles the next day. They camped 15 miles from New Orleans and early the next morning halted four miles above the city at the place Jackson had designated.

Coffee's weather-beaten men were tough, hardened veterans with the ability to take care of themselves in any emergency. They were all good shots who thought nothing of bringing down a squirrel

---

[15] Bibliotheca Parsoniana: La.-Am. MSS, No. 1019 (December 22, 1814).

from the top of the tallest tree with a rifle. They did not look very military "in their woolen hunting-shirts, of dark or dingy color, and copperas-dyed pantaloons, made, both cloth and garment, at home by their wives, mothers and sisters, with slouching wool hats, some composed of skins of raccoons and foxes, the spoils of the chase . . . with belts of untanned deer-skin, in which were stuck hunting-knives and tomahawks—with their long unkempt hair and unshorn faces." [16]

Hinds and his Dragoons came in from Woodville, Mississippi, right on the heels of Coffee's men. They had covered 230 miles in four days.

The next day, December 21, "when the orders that had been given for obstructing the different canals of the bayous below Manchac were presumed to have been executed, a detachment of the 3d regiment of militia, consisting of eight white men and a serjeant, two mulattoes and one negro, with a single boat, were sent by major Villeré [son of the owner of the plantation] to the village of the Spanish fishermen." [17]

(On that same day the British held a review of all their troops on Isle-aux-Pois. The next day Thornton and his advance guard crossed Lake Borgne and, on December 23rd, established themselves on Villeré's plantation.)

While Villeré's picket was on its way to the Spanish fishermen's village and while the British were parading on Isle-aux-Pois, Carroll arrived at the outskirts of New Orleans with 3,000 Tennesseans. His division had left Nashville on the Cumberland River on November 19. Just before they embarked, "that river, which is seldom boatable at that season of the year, was suddenly swelled by unexpected rains and torrents." [18] The flood had swept them into the Ohio and down the Mississippi in record time.

Most of Jackson's men (with the exception of Thomas and his Kentuckians who would arrive about New Year's Day) were now

---

[16] Walker, *Jackson and New Orleans*, 154-55.
[17] Latour, *Historical Memoir*, 77-78.
[18] Walker, *Jackson and New Orleans*, 155.

within a radius of four miles from the city. Coffee's Tennesseans were above the city on Avart Plantation; Plauché's battalion with Dominique You and Beluche and their gun crews were at Fort St. John; Claiborne with two regiments of Louisiana militia and Lacoste with half of the free colored battalion were on Gentilly plain;[19] the Regulars (7th and 44th) were at Fort St. Charles on the lower river corner of the city and in barracks nearby; Jugeat and his Choctaws were not far away.

In addition to these land forces, Jackson had the schooner *Carolina* and the larger *Louisiana,* a merchant vessel which was being prepared as a sloop of war. These two vessels had been transporting ammunition from the "Grand Magazine of Powder" across the river which Laffite's men kept filling.[20] The *Louisiana* was not ready for immediate action; the *Carolina* was.

The stage was now set, Jackson and his men were in the wings waiting for their cue. A preliminary one came on the evening of December 22, when Colonel Denis de Laronde of the third Louisiana militia sent Jackson word that several sails of vessels had been seen off the point of the three bayous behind Terre-aux-Boeufs. Jackson ordered engineer Lacarrière Latour and engineer Howell Tatum to find out whether or not this report were true and to examine very particularly all the communications from Terre-aux-Boeufs to Lake Borgne. They left town at eleven o'clock on the morning of Friday, December 23.

Meanwhile, Gabriel Villeré, a prisoner nine miles below New Orleans, watched and waited. Then he saw his chance. He leaped

---

[19] Claiborne complained to Jackson that he did not really know how many men were in the militia. He explained why, saying: "I have not accurate information as to the Present Condition of the Battalion of uniformed militia, at Present under your immediate orders; It has of late been much added to by Recruits from the Regular militia, and indeed *the practise* of leaving one company to join another, has of late become *so common,* that to prevent the total destruction of some corps, and much derangement, to others, I have deemed it proper to forbid it, in General militia orders." Bassett (ed.), *Correspondence,* II, 120-21.

Claiborne lacked the tact and power to make himself obeyed. Bassett, *Life of Jackson,* 158.

[20] Bassett (ed.), *Correspondence,* II, 53, 132.

through a window, jumped a picket fence and escaped in spite of shots and pursuing redcoats. Crossing the river in a small boat, he encountered Colonel de Laronde on the other side. The two found horses, galloped up the west side of the Mississippi, recrossed, and at 1:30 in the afternoon reached 106 Royal Street.

A sentinel announced the mud-spattered fugitives. " Gentlemen, what news do you bring? " asked Jackson.

" Two thousand British are on my plantation," said the excited Villeré. " More are expected. They will camp tonight and attack in strength in the morning."

" By the Eternal! " roared Old Hickory. " They shall not rest on our soil! " [21]

Meanwhile, engineers Latour and Howell Tatum had reached the boundary between Bienvenu and de Laronde plantation,[22] and had met several people hurrying to the city who told them the British were at Villeré's and that Major Villeré and others were prisoners. Tatum immediately galloped back to inform Jackson while Latour went ahead until he stepped over the boundary of Villeré's plantation from which point he watched British troops " occupying the ground from the commencement of the angle made by the road in that place to the head of the canal."

Latour was no ordinary observer. He was a man of great stature, with black eyes that illuminated the dusky skin of his big round face. His black hair and bush of beard and whiskers were streaked with white, the only indication of his forty-five years. Intelligent, astute, a graduate of the Paris Academy of Fine Arts, he was a talented engineer and architect.[23]

This Frenchman approached within rifle shot and judged the number of British to be sixteen or eighteen hundred. He noted the

---

[21] Walker, *Jackson and New Orleans*, 151.

[22] Six plantations were to be the main theater of action during the next few weeks. Beginning with Macarty and going down the river they were: Macarty, Chalmette, Bienvenu, de Laronde, Lacoste, and Villeré.

[23] Stanley Faye, " The Great Stroke of Pierre Laffite," *Louisiana Historical Quarterly*, XXIII (Baton Rouge, July, 1940), 25 in the reprint. In the spring of 1816, Latour became a Spanish spy.

position they were taking. Such exact information could not have been gained by any ordinary scout. It was then 1:30 in the afternoon. Within 25 minutes he reported at headquarters.[24]

Jackson knew he could rely on this information. He knew now that for a few hours at least he would slightly outnumber the enemy; moreover, he had the advantage of the *Carolina* and *Louisiana* and their guns. Turning to his aides he said, "Gentlemen, we must attack tonight!"

He sent couriers in all directions: to Coffee, Carroll, and Hinds above the city; to the Feliciana Dragoons on Gentilly; to Jugeat and his Choctaws, and to Plauché who was at Fort St. John. With the exception of Carroll, they were all to come with haste to Fort St. Charles where they would be inspected and provided with ammunition. Apprehending a double attack by way of Chef Menteur, Jackson sent Carroll and his whole brigade to reinforce Claiborne in the Gentilly plain.

Jackson's messengers found Patterson and Captain John Henley at Fort St. John, examining batteries being erected by Beluche's and Dominique's gun crews. The Baratarians were to hold that fort alone—Plauché and the Battalion d'Orléans were on their way to Jackson. Patterson and Henley hurried back to the city to get their ships ready to take up a position downriver opposite the enemy's camp. Because of calm, the big *Louisiana* could not steer in the stream, so Patterson instructed Lieutenant C. B. Thompson to follow when he could. Then he and Henley boarded the *Carolina* whose Baratarian crew had the ship ready to get under weigh.

After Jackson had given his orders, he ate a little rice and lay down to rest while the troops assembled. As he slept, Feliciana Dragoons scouted the enemy. They were the few horsemen whom the British subaltern had said "were checked and put to flight at the first discharge."

By 2:30 a detachment of artillery under Colonel William MacRea, with two 6-pounders commanded by Lieutenant Samuel Spotts; the

---

[24] Adams, *History of United States*, VIII, 343-44; Latour, *Historical Memoir*, 88.

7th Infantry Regiment under the command of Major Henry D. Piere; and a detachment of marines were all formed on the river road near Montreuil's plantation, the third one below the city.

At 3:00 o'clock Jackson arose, went to Fort St. Charles and stationed himself at the gate through which the troops would pass to get on the river road. Jean and Pierre Laffite, Livingston, Grymes, Duncan and Davezac were in his escort. Troops came pouring through the narrow streets and filed by them. Hinds and his Mississippi Dragoons were the first to appear. They were sent ahead to reconnoiter. Coffee and his mounted rifles came next, then the 44th Infantry, Jugeat and his Choctaws and Major Daquin's battalion of free men of color.

After them came Beale's Rifles, a corps of sixty-odd men, carrying long rifles. They were just out of sight when Jackson spied a body of men coming on the double quick down one of the side streets to the fort. "Ah! There come the brave Creoles," he cried.

Major Plauché's battalion had run all the way from Fort St. John. Jackson smiled as they passed him, then he glanced at the River. He saw that the *Carolina* was moving. It was only five o'clock, but the darkness of December night had already fallen as Jackson and his aides galloped down the road after his little army.

Most authorities estimate its strength at about 2,000. Latour's figures are:[25]

Hinds's Mississippi Mounted Rifles	107
Coffee's Tennessee Mounted Rifles	563
Beale's Rifles (lawyers and merchants)	62
Seventh U. S. Infantry	465
Forty-Fourth U. S. Infantry	331
Jugeat's Choctaws	18
Daquin's Company, Haitian colored	210
Plauché's Battalion	287
Marines	66
Light Artillery with two 6-pounders	22
	2131

[25] Latour, *Historical Memoir*, 103-104; William James, *Military Occurrences*, II, 361-62; Cooke, *Narrative of Attack on New Orleans*, 189.

Opposed to Jackson would be Colonel Thornton with the light brigade already landed which consisted of:

part of the 85th regiment of infantry	650
part of the 95th rifles—Captain Hallen	500
a detachment of sappers and miners	100
a detachment of the rocket brigade commanded by Captain Lane	80
the 4th regiment or King's own	750
	2080

On the supposition that each regiment had left a party on board to take care of the baggage, there would remain about 1,800 effectives. However, while Jackson's line was forming, the odds against him were increasing as a second brigade landed which consisted of:

21st regiment, fusileers	900
44th regiment, fusileers	750
93rd regiment, fusileers	1100
artillerists	150
	2900

Again assuming that some were left on board, 4,500 effectives had been landed on the 23rd of December before nine o'clock P. M.[26]

Jackson's line formed on De Laronde's plantation. Only one plantation, Lacoste's, separated the Americans and the British. Enemy pickets, 500 yards away, heard nothing as Jackson's troops silently took their position. Colonel de Laronde and Pierre Laffite guided Coffee, followed by Beale's Rifles and Hinds's Dragoons to the swamp side of the plantation. When the signal came, Coffee's command was to turn the British right and drive it to the river. He formed his men along the edge of the cypress swamp, perpendicular to a ditch which was the boundary of Lacoste's plantation. Coffee's men dismounted and turned their horses loose. Beale's Rifles were behind them and in the rear Hinds's Dragoons remained on their horses.

---

[26] *Ibid.*

Jackson's right formed perpendicular to the river, stretching from a boat landing on the levee along an avenue of oaks to Versailles, Colonel de Laronde's home. Artillery and marines occupied the levee road. To their left was the 7th, then Plauché's battalion and Daquin's men of color. Jugeat's Choctaws and the 44th were on Jackson's left end. Colonel Ross, the same who with Patterson had destroyed the Baratarian establishment on Grande Terre, commanded the militia battalions.

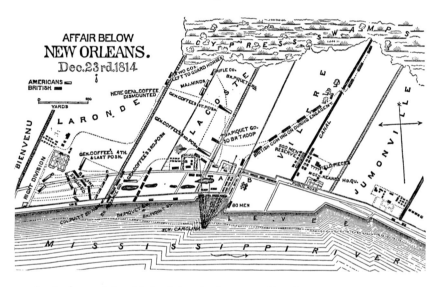

As Jackson joined his right flank two miles from the British position, Hinds's scouts reported that some of the redcoats were cooking their suppers over little fires while others were sleeping.

Because of the precedent Americans had set along the Atlantic coast, at Washington, and at Baltimore, the English acted on the supposition that no danger threatened unless they sought it. They fully expected the French and Spanish to be passive or join them. They knew there was some activity in front of them, but they were so sure it could only be Jackson's advance guard that they built their fires and moved around without the least qualm.

So secure did they feel that they paid no attention to the *Carolina* and her cargo of cannon moving downstream. They thought she was just an ordinary vessel making her usual trip down river. At 6:30 Jackson sent Livingston to Patterson to tell him to take up his position abreast the enemy camp and start bombarding it. When he sent up a red, white, and blue rocket, that would be the signal for the troops to start firing.

The *Carolina* carried five 6-pounders on each broadside and two long twelves on pivots, one foreward and the other aft. Her broadside then, would be seven guns: two twelves and five sixes. Her crew of 90 men were mostly Baratarians, skilled in the use of cannon.

At 7:30 the *Carolina* was in position and ready to fire. All was quiet in the British camp. Suddenly the redcoats heard a shout rising out of the waters of the Mississippi: " Now, damn their eyes, give it 'em! " [27]

All Hell broke loose, or so thought the confounded British as a storm of 6-pound shot and grape flashed down on them " like so many thunder-bolts, the balls boring down whole piles of arms, knocking kettles off the fires, scattering blazing beams of wood about, maiming some soldiers, and sending others whence no traveller returns. . . . The levee being only three feet above the level of the water, was no screen. . . . Round after round, and ball after ball, were vomited forth, driving the troops into most dire confusion, which caused a ten-fold panic during the darkness, and the confusion beggars all description; no mob could be in a more utter state of disorganization. . . . Officers were buckling on their swords, and throwing down knives and forks, and calling on their soldiers. Soldiers were looking after their arms or buckling on their knapsacks, and calling to their officers. Bugle-horns were sounding, while the soldiers were striving to gather together . . . all the time under the fire of this floating battery at point-blank range, and without any effective aim to silence these seven noisy monsters, the fire of which was assisted, when some of the fires were extinguished, by the confusion of voices amongst the soldiers." [28]

[27] Cooke, *Narrative of Attack*, 191.
[28] *Ibid.*, 191-92.

Colonel Thornton, probably the most able British officer, kept his head. He ordered the 95th to rush to the support of its pickets along the river, and the 85th to support its outposts spread across Lacoste's plantation to the right of the 95th. The 4th or King's own was sent back to Villeré's house to act as reserve.

The *Carolina* fired seven broadsides in rapid succession, then sent up the red, white, and blue rocket signal. Jackson's sector was in motion. Lieutenant Spotts with his artillery supported by 60 marines had moved down the road next the levee. Major Piere, leading the 7th, was moving in column. Jackson was near the 7th. Ross's brigade—Plauché's battalion, Daquin's colored, and the 44th led by Major Baker—marched in extended line. This was all right at first, but soon the river inclined to the left and pushed the 7th inward on Plauché's battalion while on the other side De Laronde's house and a grove of orange trees pressed the 44th against Daquin's men. Thus Plauché and Daquin with their commands were pushed back of the line. This could not be corrected because of darkness and the momentum of the advance.

Colonel Piatt and a company of the 7th had by this time filed through a gate of De Laronde's plantation and advanced as far as the boundary of Lacoste's plantation when an outpost of the enemy—80 men of the 95th Rifles under Captain Hallen—opened fire. Hallen's men were in a ditch behind a fence. The 7th and 44th moved in the direction of the fire and forced them to retire. Meanwhile, the artillery blazed away. The British, reinforced by more of the 95th, regained their position and started for the two guns. The marines recoiled under their heavy fire. Wounded horses overturned one of the guns. " Save the guns, boys! " yelled Jackson.[29]

Part of the 7th dashed forward, rescued the marines and guns, and drove back the enemy. Because of numerous ditches, the red-coats were able to reform. Seeing the 44th weakened, they attacked

---

[29] Jackson would later say, when complimented on the gracefulness of his bow, that he learned the art on the night of the twenty-third when, though the British thought differently, he never wasted so much politeness in his life in bowing to their bullets as they whistled around his head. Walker, *Jackson and New Orleans*, 172.

it. The 44th was mostly young boys. Plauché's Creoles and Daquin's Haitians rushed from behind and with the 44th drove the British back.

Jackson's right wing had been in action about an hour when he sent a scout to discover Coffee's position. He had not as yet had any news from his left wing. Coffee, meanwhile, had deployed his men next the swamp and was opposite the *Carolina* when she sent up her rocket signal. With his dismounted and Beale's Rifles parallel to the river, he started west like a broom toward the enemy. Hinds's cavalry remained in the rear—they would ruin their horses if they attempted, in the dark, to maneuver over terrain cut up with ditches and bayous.

The 85th was closer to Coffee than he had expected—it had retired two or three hundred yards into the open field where darkness was some protection from the belching *Carolina*. Coffee had advanced only 100 yards when the 85th opened fire. He had ordered his men not to fire unless they were sure of felling an object. Their aim was accurate; they fired faster than the redcoats. The 85th retreated, rallied and charged, and retreated again until they reached an orange grove. Here they formed to fight. Coffee's men were overpowering them when four companies of the 21st Royal North British Fusileers came up from the boats.

The subaltern said: " There cannot be a doubt that we should have fallen to a man had not the arrival of fresh troops at this critical juncture turned the tide of affairs." [30]

The reinforcements formed for battle. Their fire revealed their position. Coffee's men charged, forced them toward the river. Beale's Rifles had been separated from Coffee by a fence. When Coffee moved right, Rifles on the extreme left did not observe the movement because of gun smoke and darkness. They kept going straight ahead and found themselves in a trap.

Some of the British 85th had been very quiet, catching their breath after Coffee turned to the right. They saw a small column

---

[30] *A Subaltern in America*, 1833 Philadelphia edition, 225.

advancing toward them. The subaltern said: " We were at this time amply supported by other troops . . . and willing to annihilate the corps now approaching. We forbade the men to fire till it should be mingled with us. We did even more than this. Opening a passage for them through our center we permitted some hundred and twenty men to march across our ditch, and then wheeling up with a loud shout, we completely enclosed them. Never have I witnessed a panic more perfect or more sudden than that which seized them. They no sooner beheld the snare into which they had fallen, than with one voice they cried aloud for quarter; and they were to a man made prisoners on the spot. The reader will smile when he is informed that the little corps thus captured consisted mainly of members of the legal profession. The barristers, attorneys and notaries of New Orleans . . . were all made prisoners. The circumstance was productive of no trifling degree of mirth amongst us; and to do them justice, the poor lawyers, as soon as they recovered from their first alarm, joined heartily in our laughter." [31]

By this time Coffee had most of the 85th on the run toward the river. They took refuge behind sections of an old levee. Thick fog from the river obscured everything. Coffee wanted to charge, but one of his officers had discovered the advantage of the British and persuaded Coffee it would be too hazardous, that the enemy " could be driven no further, and would, from the point they occupied, resist with the bayonet, and repel with considerable loss, any attempt that might be made to dislodge them." [32] Furthermore, Coffee's men would be exposed to fire from the *Carolina.*

At this point Jackson's messenger reached Coffee and told him that Jackson feared the consequences, under the circumstances, of further prosecution of a night attack on troops then acting together for the first time. Coffee was to withdraw to the position on De Laronde's plantation where he had been when the battle started.

The battle had raged for an hour and a half over one square mile of plantation fields and ditches. In the obscurity of gun smoke and

---

[31] *Ibid.,* 226-27.
[32] Eaton, *Life of Jackson,* 315.

fog, " such confusion took place as seldom occurs in war—the bayonet of the British and the knife of the American were in active opposition at close quarters during this eventful night. . . . The darkness was partially dispelled for a few moments, now and then, by flashes of fire-arms; and whenever the outlines of men were distinguishable, the Americans called out ' don't fire, we are your friends!' prisoners were taken and retaken. The Americans were litigating and wrangling, and protesting that they were not taken fairly, and were hugging their fire-arms and bewailing their separation from a favourite rifle that they wished to retain as their lawful property."

" The British soldiers likewise, hearing their mother tongue spoken, were captured by this deception; when such mistakes being detected, the nearest American received a knock-down blow; and in this manner prisoners on both sides having escaped, again joined in the fray, calling out lustily for their respective friends." [33]

So Coffee retired to the swamp end of De Laronde's plantation and Jackson's right wing to the main entrance of that plantation near the river. Meanwhile, 350 Louisiana Militia under General David Morgan who were stationed at English Turn (seven or eight miles below the British) knew the redcoats were on Villeré's plantation almost as soon as Jackson did. They wanted to attack immediately, but Morgan refused to give the order since he did not know Jackson's wishes. When the night battle started and they heard the firing, Morgan could restrain his men no longer; so he gave the necessary orders and led them through muddy roads and darkness to Jumonville's plantation which was immediately below Villeré's.

It was about 11:30 when some of his scouts came across enemy outposts and fired. The fire was returned. Then Morgan ordered his men into a field until they could reconnoiter. They were unable to learn anything and at three o'clock they started back to their post at English Turn.

During the night opposing generals estimated their losses. Keane officially reported the British losses at 46 killed, 167 wounded and

[33] Cooke, *Narrative of Attack*, 195.

64 missing.[34] Jackson's losses were 24 killed, 115 wounded and 74 prisoners.[35]

At four o'clock on the morning of December 24, Jackson began to move his army back to Rodriguez Canal between Chalmette and Macarty plantations. Carroll with 1,000 of his men was already there. Jackson knew the British were 6,000 strong and that more troops were still coming up the bayous.

He did not know that on that day, the day before Christmas, British and American peace commissioners were signing a peace treaty at Ghent in Belgium. It provided for the *status quo ante bellum.* The British interpreted this to mean that before the war Louisiana did not belong to the United States; therefore, Louisiana's future status would be determined after the invasion force had rolled into New Orleans and up the Mississippi valley.

The British peace commissioners could not know that Jackson's night attack, the opening round in the Battle of New Orleans, had convinced Major General Keane and Admiral Cochrane that the army defending the city was really larger than it was. Therefore, they would wait until their force assembled in all its power and majesty before attacking the " backwoods rabble."

The delay gave Jackson time to dig a ditch.

---

[34] Keane's report, December 26, 1814, cited in Adams, *History of United States,* VIII, 350-51. *A Subaltern in America,* 1826 Philadelphia edition, 292, says the British loss was enormous, that not less than 500 men had fallen.

[35] Latour, *Historical Memoir,* 102-103; Adams, *History of United States,* VIII, 350-51.

SIR EDWARD

MICHAEL PAKENHAM

THERE WAS NO FIGHTING ON THE 24TH. JACKSON DECIDED IT would be foolhardy to send his troops, most of whom had no bayonets, against six or seven thousand redcoats skilled in the use of them.[1] No, there was too much danger on the open plain. His men needed something to shield them. They could dig out the old grass-grown Rodriguez Canal and throw up the mud into breastworks.

Old Hickory requisitioned every spade, shovel, axe, saw, wheelbarrow, cart, and wagon in New Orleans. Hundreds of slaves

---

[1] " It had been Jackson's anxious desire to renew at daybreak the conflict, which night had interrupted, and to attack the British vigorously. But he learned from scouts, that the English Major-General Keane . . . had received a reinforcement of 3500 men. Jackson was, nevertheless, as much as ever disposed to assail the English with his small force of inexperienced militia, but his aide, Livingston, very prudently advised him to consult Major St. Gème. The latter had gone about a good deal with Moreau, when the latter visited New Orleans a few years before, and had examined its situation with the critical eye of a tactician; had studied its capabilities for defence in case of hostile attack, and, hence, was peculiarly fitted to give Jackson some excellent advice. This he did, and had the great merit of making Jackson comprehend that Keane, with his 6,000 men, would, in the open field, surround, defeat, and capture him and his small force of raw levies, who had not much more of the soldier about them than the mere name; he then pointed out the canal or channel . . . behind which we had assumed our position, as the very spot that Moreau himself had indicated as the best one adapted to a defence of the city, particularly by unpractised troops. Jackson listened to this advice." Nolte, *Fifty Years in Both Hemispheres*, 213.

helped in the hand-blistering work.[2] While Mississippi and Feliciana horsemen patrolled the fields in front of Jackson, and while the *Carolina* kept up an irritating fire, work progressed on the barricade which extended from the river to the cypress swamp. Empty barrels and sugar casks were lined up at intervals along Rodriguez Canal and the apertures between them filled with earth. This formed a temporary screen. The canal, ten feet wide, protected the barricade in front.[3]

After deepening the ditch three feet, the toilers struck water and the excavated soil began sliding back into the canal. Cypress logs were cut (from the plentiful stand nearby) and laid crib fashion. Dirt was hauled in from some distance to thicken the watery mud which was thrown into the cribs. Slowly the mud piles grew. By nightfall they were three and four feet high the whole length of the line. As the ditch was deepened in the week that followed, Jackson's parapet on its outer face (including the depth of the ditch) was everywhere at least seven feet, and in many places eight feet high.[4]

Throughout the 24th the British made no move. Perhaps Major General Keane was waiting to shift responsibility to the commander in chief who was on his way. The *Louisiana*, the *Carolina*, and Jackson's road battery were not insuperable obstacles. On this day Keane could have marched his troops along the cypress swamp— one mile from the ships and Jackson's two sixes—to New Orleans. Jackson's barricade was in its infancy and open behind. But Keane preferred to keep his troops under an irritating fire.

By the next morning, Christmas, all the British troops from Isle-aux-Pois had been landed. Their chief occupation seemed to be eying the *Carolina* " whose sides still smoked by day, and at night vomited iron harbingers from its port into the bivouac of the British, so that the city of New Orleans and General Jackson now became only a secondary consideration, and the discussion was how to get rid of this watery dragon." [5]

---

[2] Buell, *History of Jackson*, I, 400-402.
[3] Cooke, *Narrative of Attack*, 201-202.

[4] Buell, *History of Jackson*, I, 401.
[5] Cooke, *Narrative of Attack*, 201.

Then cannon shots broke the quiet of Christmas day. Ditchdiggers dropped their shovels and ran for cover. Jackson sent Hinds to find out the cause of the disturbance. He returned to say that the British were jubilant, a new commander had arrived from England, someone very important, perhaps the Duke of Wellington himself.

"Who's afraid of the Iron Duke?" shouted Old Hickory. "Here we shall dig our stakes and not abandon them until we drive the red coats away. Men, get back to your shovels." [6]

The new commander was not the Iron Duke but his brother-in-law, Major General Sir Edward Michael Pakenham, the second most popular military commander in England. (This was the same Pakenham who had already had his neck adjusted twice by French Creoles.) Major General Samuel Gibbs, second in command, an efficient staff, and 3,000 reinforcements came with Pakenham. When they had left England at the end of October, English and American commissioners at Ghent were in their third month of peace negotiations.

Rumor had already spread among the English troops that Sir Edward had in his dispatch case a commission as governor of Louisiana and the promise of an earldom when he occupied that province. [7]

It was not British policy to reward and maintain such meritorious but penniless conquerors as Sir Edward with money from England. Pakenham's earldom would be supported by the $15,000,000 in cotton, sugar, corn, and whiskey in New Orleans warehouses. This wealth would be used to dazzle Louisianians with the splendor of British pageantry. The merchant fleet would carry this wealth to England.

---

[6] Walker, *Jackson and New Orleans*, 211.

[7] There was a lady on board one of the ships in Lake Borgne who expected to become the " governess " of Louisiana. Letter of Pierre Favrot to his wife, January 21, 1815, Howard-Tilton Memorial Library, New Orleans. The author is indebted to Connie G. Griffith for her typed transcript of this letter. She asked, " Who was the lady? " The author could only point out that Pakenham was not married. He had been engaged to Lady Milbanke, but she had jilted him when she learned there was insanity in the family. At that very moment Lady Milbanke was getting ready to marry Lord Byron, who had a club foot. They were married one week later, January 2, 1814.

Once established, the system would work—as it was working in India. Mississippi Valley cotton would be manufactured into cloth and sent back for the natives to buy at England's price. Here was a splendid opportunity for many Englishmen to make their fortunes. One officer on Villeré's plantation saw the situtation thus: "The conquest of New Orleans would have proved the most valuable acquisition that could be made to the British dominions, throughout the whole western hemisphere. In possession of that post, we should have kept the entire southern trade of the United States in check; and furnished means of commerce to our own merchants, of incalculable value." [8]

Pakenham rode forth to survey his encampment and the position of the Americans. He could see nothing of Jackson's army except Hinds's horsemen galloping over the cane-stubble fields in very unmilitary fashion. They would rush up to British outposts, shoot as they whizzed by, then yell like savages and wheel in the opposite direction. Pakenham looked toward New Orleans but "the town was completely hid, nor was it possible to see beyond the distance of a very few miles, either in front or rear, so flat and unbroken was the face of the country." [9]

Pakenham called his staff together in Villeré's house and gave vent to his feelings. "With the forces at our disposal," he said, "our entrance into New Orleans should have been swift and easy. I regret the defeat of our forces due to the error made on the 23rd of December. Our troops should have advanced to New Orleans immediately on taking Villeré's plantation. However, that is past. Let us look to our present position. I do not like it. Never have troops been found in so strange a position, the Mississippi from eight hundred to a thousand yards in breadth on our left flank, an impassable wood on our right, the Americans less than three-quarters of a mile in front, and the fleet only supplying enough boats to carry off one-third of the force collected on this spot." [10]

---

[8] Gleig, *Campaigns of British Army*, 1836 London edition, 385.
[9] *Ibid.*, 1826 London edition, 303.
[10] Cooke, *Narrative of Attack*, 203.

Admiral Cochrane interrupted angrily, " We were not defeated," he cried, " and there is nothing wrong with our position. If the army shrinks from attack here, I will bring up my sailors and marines from the fleet. We will storm the American lines and march into the city. Then the soldiers can bring up the baggage." [11]

Stung by this taunt, Pakenham gave up the idea of changing the theater of operations. His next suggestion met with better success. It was to bring guns from the ships and blow the *Carolina* from the water. Then the British could make a formidable display of military power and discipline which would overwhelm the " backwoods rabble."

And so Sir Edward, instead of making an instantaneous attack, " set himself down to lay siege to the American schooner, the destruction of which had no more to do with the capture of New Orleans than the most foreign thing in nature; besides, a ship with more guns lay higher up the river to dispute the further march to the city *by the road*. . . . There was no harm in blowing both of them up as soon as possible, but there was no occasion for the whole army to await the event; for while time was lost in disposing of these annoyances, the barricade was rising out of the earth like enchantment as a real stoppage to take the place of an imaginary one." [12]

All that day and the next sailors labored with incredible toil in December cold and rain to bring nine field pieces, two howitzers, one mortar, a furnace for heating balls, and a supply of ammunition from the ships in Lake Borgne, sixty miles away, and then up the bayou and through mud to the river bank.

On Christmas Day Jackson sent orders to General Morgan to evacuate his position at English Turn. He was to send a garrison of 100 men with the artillery across the river to Fort St. Leon. The rest of his men were to cross the river also, but they were to ascend its right bank and go into camp opposite Jackson's line on the plantation of " big fat Dr. Flood."

---

[11] *Ibid.*, 212.
[12] *Ibid.*, 203-204.

The river was rising. This gave Jackson an idea. He sent engineers to cut the levee both above and below Villeré's plantation. Water began to flow through the cut, then the river fell. Instead of flooding the British camp, the cuts let enough water into canals and bayous so that it was easier for the enemy to bring heavy artillery up the waterways.

Winter rains chilled both camps. Jackson kept his men busy at the ditch. He was surveying the work next the cypress swamp when Jean Laffite pointed out that the line was not long enough, that it should be carried through the cypress woods and into the swamp itself. Otherwise, the enemy might turn the left end of Jackson's line.[13]

Old Hickory agreed with Jean, so engineers directed men to anchor logs to trees for a platform behind whatever barrier they could erect. Meanwhile, Jackson had no regular chain of outposts like the British. But, every morning before daylight, mounted horsemen spread themselves over the plain to watch British movements.

At night Jackson's "rabbit hunters" took over with their own special system of irritation that made night hideous for the British. They stalked and killed sentinels and picked off officers going the rounds. Worse still, groups would silently approach an outpost, fire simultaneously, and drive in. Then they would lie on their bellies in the cane stubble, convulsed with silent mirth at they watched developments. The aroused British would form in column and prepare to meet the whole American army. After all, it *had* attacked at night on the 23rd. Then the officers would discover there was no army in front of them, and command the soldiers to lie down, only to arouse them again and again because of the same false alarm.

Officers complained bitterly of this unsportsmanlike conduct. "Those savages have no knowledge of how war should be fought," whined one of them. "In Europe, when two armies face each other, the outposts of neither are molested. Nay, so far is this tacit good understanding carried out that I myself have seen French and English

---

[13] Bassett (ed.), *Correspondence*, II, 125.

sentinels not more than twenty yards apart. These ' dirty shirts ' entertain no such chivalric notions." [14]

What that English officer failed to understand was that the " dirty shirts " could not afford to have chivalric notions such as his. The " dirty shirts " were by now three thousand citizens contending against ten thousand veteran soldiers and marines come to murder, and seize the produce of their peaceful industry so that Pakenham could establish himself in pomp and glory as their master and make them slaves of England.

On the evening of December 26, Hinds reported to Jackson, saying, " Enemy batteries on the levee seem to be completed."

Jackson notified Patterson and he sent word to Captain Henley to get the *Carolina* up river out of danger. Captain Henley made every possible exertion to move the vessel, but without success " the wind being N. N. W. and blowing fresh, and too scant to get under weigh, and the current too rapid to move her by warping." [15]

The Macarty mansion, one hundred yards behind his ditch, was Jackson's headquarters. His best observation post was from a second story window of the mansion. At daylight on the morning of December 27, Jackson was stationed there with a spy glass an old Frenchman had sent him. He looked for the *Carolina*. She was near the far bank of the river but still opposite the British camp. The *Louisiana* was closer to the American position, still she was only one mile above the *Carolina* and within range of British guns.

Suddenly Jackson saw, and then heard those guns concentrate their fire on the *Carolina*. The bombardment knocked down the bulwarks, rigging and spars. Hot shot lodged in the schooner's main hold under her cables in such a way that sailors could not quench the burning cables. The cabin and filling room contained a considerable quantity of powder. Expecting every moment that the *Carolina* would blow up, Henley reluctantly gave orders for the crew to

---

[14] Gleig, *Campaigns of British Army*, 1836 London edition, 313-14.
[15] Henley to Patterson, New Orleans, December 28, 1814, Master Commandant's Letters.

abandon her. This was effected with the loss of one killed and six wounded. A short time after Henley " had the extreme mortification of seeing her blow up." [16]

English and American soldiers lined the levee watching the destruction. Among the crowd of spectators were the Indian chiefs who appeared deeply interested in the proceedings.[17] Then the *Carolina* blew up, the redcoats shouted and yelled in glee. They had suffered four days from that terrible floating battery.

Meantime, Lieutenant C. C. B. Thompson was straining every nerve to get the *Louisiana* beyond reach of British batteries. She was loaded with powder.[18] Wind and current were against her. Americans and British and their Indian allies saw the Baratarians get into boats, fasten two lines, take up oars. Tensely they waited. Then a great shout escaped the Americans as they saw the *Louisiana* move. Baratarians towed her beyond reach of the enemy.

The British were foiled again! And because of their own error. They should have opened fire on the *Louisiana* first, then they could have taken care of the *Carolina*. Charred timber of this vessel had well-nigh reached the Gulf of Mexico before Pakenham took the offensive.

During the night of the 27th he established batteries on the river road and formed his phalanx into two brigades.[19] These brigades moved in the dark across De Laronde's plantation. By superiority of numbers they obliged Jackson's advance guard to fall back. Old Hickory had ordered Colonel MacRea, commander of artillery, to fire and blow up all the buildings on Chalmette and Bienvenu so they could no longer protect the enemy from artillery fire. MacRea and his outfit succeeded in destroying all the buildings on Chalmette

---

[16] *Ibid.*

[17] Hill, *Recollections of an Artillery Officer*, 328.

[18] Latour, *Historical Memoir*, 114.

[19] One brigade under Gibbs consisted of the 4th, 21st, and 44th Regiments and the 5th West India black corps; the other under Keane consisted of the 85th and 93rd Regiments, the remains of the 95th Rifle Corps, and the 1st West India black corps. A squadron of the 14th light dragoons and the artillery were to support Keane. Cooke, *Narrative of Attack*, 206; Gleig, *Campaigns of the British*, 1836 London edition, 312.

and were stuffing those on Bienvenu with combustibles when they heard the British coming and escaped without being detected.

Meanwhile, Jean Laffite had returned to the Macarty mansion from an inspection of the powder and shot supply. Perhaps it was he who convinced Jackson that Beluche and Dominique You, the best cannoneers in the western hemisphere, should not be used any longer for sentry duty at Fort St. John. At any rate, Jackson sent for them to come immediately to the mud ramparts.

As Jean Laffite supervised the installation of two twenty-fours, the number of cannon on the American line increased to five. The two 6-pounders used on the 23rd were designated Battery No. 1 and placed on the levee. A 6-pound howitzer, Battery No. 2, was planted so that it commanded the river road. Laffite's two twenty-fours, fifty yards from No. 2, became Batteries No. 3 and No. 4.[20]

As the gun emplacements were being built, a French engineer had suggested filling up the hollowed redoubts with cotton bales three or four deep.[21] Wooden platforms could then be placed over them and made secure for heavy cannon. The crenellated openings on both sides of the redoubt could be constructed with six or eight bales fastened to the main body of the redoubt by iron rings.

Jackson approved this plan and his men seized the nearest supply which was on a ship that had been loaded before the invasion. Most of the cotton belonged to Vincent Nolte. When he recognized his marks on the bales he was somewhat vexed at the use made of his good cotton. He told Livingston that there was plenty of cheaper cotton in town which should have been used. Livingston replied, " Well, Mr. Nolte, if this is your cotton, you at least will not think it any hardship to defend it." [22]

At daybreak on the morning of December 28, Pakenham's troops

---

[20] It is difficult to be accurate about these batteries. Latour makes the 6-pounders and the howitzer Battery No. 1. He does not mention a Battery No. 4 for the 28th of December. *Historical Memoir*, 122; Parton, *Life of Jackson*, II, 136; Walker, *Jackson and New Orleans*, 226.

[21] Perhaps the French engineer was H. S. Bonneval Latrobe. Latour, *Historical Memoir*, 120.

[22] Nolte, *Fifty Years in Both Hemispheres*, 215-16.

formed in order of attack. Gibbs placed his brigade in column along the cypress wood throwing out skirmishers halfway across the plain. Keane did the same with his troops along the river road. His men were preceded by several pieces of artillery and his right was covered by the rifle corps which in extended order met the skirmishers from Gibbs's line.

The frosty morning was clear and bright. In spite of harrassment during the night by " dirty shirts," expectations of success were high as the whole army started to move. On it went without any halt or hindrance, but as it came from behind the buildings on Bienvenu, it was not unseen.

Jackson had been at his observation post before dawn, waiting for the first streak of light. Hinds had informed him that enemy guns were in position and the army on the move. Jackson was relieved and thrilled when he saw Dominique and Beluche with their gun crew coming on the run, their red shirts stained with perspiration and splattered with mud. Gambie, Chighizola, and Raymond Ranchier were among the crew. Clowning, joking, they loped easily along. Men on the line cheered them, but the Baratarians did not pause; they went right to work swabbing and charging the twenty-four at No. 3.

Behind them came the Baratarian crew of the destroyed *Carolina*. They were in two groups, one under Lieutenant Crawley and the other under Lieutenant Norris. Crawley's group manned the howitzer and Norris and his Baratarians took over the twenty-four at No. 4.[23]

Jackson saw that the *Louisiana* had moved a little way downstream and anchored so that her guns would command the whole field in front of his line. Then he saw Hinds's observation corps falling back and the British coming from behind the Bienvenu plantation buildings, their bright colored uniforms and shiny muskets glittering in the winter sunlight. The whole army was in two strong columns: one by the river and one by the swamp. The swamp!

---

[23] Walker, *Jackson and New Orleans*, 226-27; Parton, *Life of Jackson*, II, 136.

Jackson's weakest sector! The ditch there was only a couple of feet wide and the breastworks were barely noticeable.

Jackson raced down the steps and ran to his horse. Abner Duncan galloped up and stopped him before he could ride away. " The legislature is going to give up the country to the British," shouted Duncan. " Governor Claiborne wants to know what to do." (According to Marigny, Jackson had forbidden Claiborne to come to camp.) [24]

" Tell him to investigate. If he finds this is true, tell him to blow up the legislature," yelled Jackson as he raced against time along his line. He saw Jugeat who by now had nearly sixty Choctaws. " Get into the swamp," ordered Jackson. He knew the Choctaws could maneuver on logs like alligators.

It was 8:25 when enemy field artillery opened up with shells, hot shot, and Congreve rockets.[25] " Dirty shirts " and " rabbit hunters " had never seen Congreve rockets before. Pakenham expected to frighten them and throw them in confusion. The Americans were used to bullets which they could not see coming but which hummed as they passed. But the rockets were a different matter. Each rocket made a roaring swoosh. The " swooping thing was dreadfully personal. It appeared to be darting directly at each watching soldier, making him shake in his boots, turning his knees to water. Only when he saw it strike the ground some distance in front could he believe it was not aimed at him. Even then the menace of the thing with a pointed iron head and an eight-foot stick was not ended. Smoking and sputtering, it writhed through the grass like a serpent.

---

[24] *Reflection on the Campaign*, 5.

[25] As early as 1232, Chinese had used rockets in warfare, firing them from bamboo tubes. As cannon developed, rockets declined. However, in the 18th century they were used in India against the British. Sir William Congreve became interested in this recoilless weapon and improved it. Wellington used more than 20,000 Congreve rockets in 1807 when he beseiged and burned Copenhagen. Congreve rockets made their American debut at the Battle of Lundy's Lane in July, 1814. They were used at Bladensburg in August. Francis Scott Key, watching the bombardment of Fort McHenry on the morning of September 13 " in the rocket's red glare," saw " bombs bursting in air." Fairfax Downey, *Sound of Guns* (New York, 1955), 68-77.

Then a time fuse burst its black powder charge with a sharp report and a spurt of acrid smoke." [26]

Congreve rockets rained down between the first line at Rodriguez Canal and the second line on Canal Dupré. Jackson placed them in their proper place when he yelled, " Pay no attention to the rockets boys, they are mere toys to amuse children." [27]

For a moment there was no reply from the Americans. Jackson's aides had warned his men to hold their fire. The enemy came nearer and nearer. Then suddenly the *Louisiana* and the four land batteries let loose. Cannon balls, striking Keane's column, knocked down soldiers and tossed them into the air like old bags. One single ball from the *Louisiana* killed fifteen men. Jackson's batteries stopped enemy field artillery, killing or wounding all the gunners. Red-hot shot struck the buildings beside Keane's men and set them on fire. Blazing wood scorched panic-stricken soldiers as bright uniforms flattened in the mud of plantation ditches.

The British column by the swamp had better luck. Gibbs had no respect for what he described with contempt as the " mere rudiments of an entrenched camp." Why, his men could easily jump that miserable ditch!

A detachment of Carroll's riflemen came out from behind the breastworks—they were itching for action. British rifles, concealed in the edge of the swamp, killed five and wounded eight. Then Jugeat and his Choctaws came to the rescue. They leaped lightly from one log to another, came upon the British from behind, fired their rifles at short range. Redcoats peered into the moss-draped cypress forest. Not an Indian could they see. Colonel Rennie led his rifles away from the swamp and was about to turn Carroll's flank when Gibbs sent him word that Pakenham had commanded a retreat. Both Gibbs and Rennie were disgusted. They knew they could have overcome the Tennesseans and gotten behind Jackson's line.

Pakenham had ordered his proud army to retire, but how? File

---

[26] *Ibid.*, 71-72.
[27] Walker, *Jackson and New Orleans*, 257; M'Afee, *History of Late War*, 514.

to the rear in small squads as rapidly as possible. Jackson's gunners were watching. Jeering, booing, they shot at each running group; never missing their mark. One 9-pound shot hit a retreating soldier on the knapsack and dashed him to pieces. Captain Collings got up from the ditch where he was lying and took only a few steps before a cannon ball struck his head and knocked it off his shoulders.[28]

Seven hours passed before the cannoneers relented and ceased firing. Seven hours of lying low in wet ditches did something to the mud-soaked survivors who had boasted they would sleep in New Orleans that night. They were glad when the shades of night concealed their humiliation from prisoners and slaves.

"Thus, without as much as one effort to force through them, was a British army baffled and repulsed by a horde of raw militiamen, ranged in line behind a mud wall, which could have hardly protected them from musketry, far less from round-shot. There was not a man among us," said the subaltern, "who failed to experience both shame and indignation, when he found himself retreating before a force for which he entertained the most sovereign contempt." [29]

No official British report was published concerning the killed and wounded on that day, December 28. Most estimates placed the number of casualties at 200. Considering that the only weapons used by the Americans were those of the artillery, the chances are that few of the wounded ever recovered. The American loss was nine killed and eight wounded.[30]

Patterson praised the Baratarian gunners in his report to the Secretary of the Navy saying: "You will have learned from my former letters that the crew of the Louisiana is composed of men of all nations (English excepted) taken from the streets of New Orleans not a fortnight before the battle, yet I never knew guns better served, or a more animated fire, than was supported from her."

---

[28] *A Subaltern in America*, 1833 Philadelphia edition, 235-36.
[29] *Ibid.*, 235.
[30] Walker, *Jackson and New Orleans*, 233.

But, in his very next sentence, the commodore belittled this praise when he attributed the skill and bravery of the Baratarians to Lieutenant C. C. B. Thompson, who, said Patterson, " deserves great credit for the discipline to which in so short a time he had brought such men, two-thirds of whom do not understand English." [31]

Those Baratarians would have known what to do even without direction from Lieutenant Thompson. They probably gave their own orders—in French. The British had been very much astonished on the night of the first attack, to hear the word of command given in French; for they did not expect the French inhabitants would fight against them.[32]

Only yankees sent in reports to the War Department and to the Navy Department concerning the Battle of New Orleans. They mentioned by name only Anglo-Saxon Americans. Jackson, in his general orders and in a very few of his letters, did mention Creoles by name.

When the fire of battle had ceased on December 28, Jackson returned to his headquarters at Macarty house and found Marigny with " a heart enraged " waiting for him. Marigny had gone to the legislature about eleven o'clock that morning and had met Magloire Guichard, Speaker of the House, coming down the steps with tears rolling down his cheeks.

" We are accused of treason," he said, " the doors of the legislature are closed by order of General Jackson."

Jackson listened patiently to Marigny's story of what had happened. Then he took Marigny by the hand and said: " Return to the city. Reassure your colleagues. It is all a misunderstanding. I was occupied in fighting when I sent word to Governor Claiborne to blow up the legislature if he was sure it wanted to capitulate." [33]

One cannot read the record of the investigation which followed

---

[31] Patterson to Secretary of Navy, United States ship *Louisiana*, four miles below New Orleans, December 29, 1814, Master Commandant's Letters, Vol. II, 1814.

[32] Letter from a Yankee to his " Dear Brother," written December 30, 1814, Boston *Daily Advertiser and Repertory*, February 4, 1815.

[33] Marigny, *Reflection on the Campaign*, 5-6.

without feeling that there were some "summer soldiers and sun-
shine patriots" in the legislature. Only four of its members were
at the front.[34] A faction of the legislature was concerned about the
rumor that Jackson would fire the city if the British drove him back.
This group was ready to capitulate to the British rather than see
the wealth in their warehouses destroyed. If they did not remember,
British agents reminded them that "loyalists" had been well repaid
during the revolution of the thirteen colonies. Take the case of
Benedict Arnold. He had received 6,315 pounds in cash, an annual
pension of 500 pounds for his wife, army commissions for his three
oldest sons, and pensions of 100 pounds each for his five youngest
children.[35]

Neither Jackson nor Claiborne considered the charge of treason
as being very serious. The next day the legislature was in session
as though nothing unusual had happened.

---

[34] "We regret not knowing the name of one of these persons: those we have learned
are general Garrique Flojack, major Eziel, and Mr. Bufort." John Reid and John Henry
Eaton, *The Life of Andrew Jackson* (Philadelphia, 1817), 322. The fourth was Sebastian
Hiriard of the Senate "who served a considerable time in the ranks of the volunteer
battalion, and afterwards as adjutant of the colored troops." Jackson's address to the
army, January 21, 1815, *Niles' Register*, VII (February 25, 1815), 404.

[35] Richard B. Morris, editor, *Encyclopedia of American History* (2 vols., New York,
1953), I, 104. British magazines published Arnold's address of October 7, 1780, in
which he explained why he could not be silent as to the motives which induced him to
join the king's arms. The editor of *Niles' Register* pointed out the resemblance of
a number of passages "to a multitude of speeches, essays, and paragraphs of the present
day. . . . Indeed one might be inclined to think that several of our orators had borrowed
their ideas from Benedict: his abuse of congress, his terror of France, his eulogies on
Great Britain." *Niles' Register*, V (January 29, 1814), 357-58.

THE ARTILLERY DUEL,

JANUARY 1

JACKSON COULD AFFORD TO BE MAGNANIMOUS WITH THE LEGIS-
lature. His army had won victories; its elation knew no bounds.
His troops were " so warm for the attack " that he had to make a
speech to them to keep them quiet. One soldier, writing to his
brother, said: "Although the New Orleans troops are constantly
under arms, such is the spirit which prevails among them, that they
submit to the fatigues of the camp with the greatest cheerfulness,
and it appears more like a party of pleasure, than the encampment
of an army in hourly expectation of being led into battle. The
Tennessee troop are equally brave and confident of success with
those from the city, and the French and Americans appear to vie
which shall give each other the most praise. Indeed, an Aid-de-camp
of the general said he could not get a man of them to stop to keep
clear of the shot and rockets which were flying among them. They
volunteer and go out in parties of 20 or 30 men, and pick off the
British when they get a chance. . . . The deserters say that there
would be a great many more desert, if they were not afraid of
' those fellows with dirty shirts,' but soon as they see any coming
up to them, they shoot them with their rifles, so that many of the
deserters cannot get near enough to our pickets to cry out *a friend.*" [1]

---

[1] Unsigned letter to " Dear Brother," Boston *Daily Advertiser and Repertory,*
February 4, 1815.

By night, rabbit hunters varied their tactics. Sometimes they carted 6-pounders within cannon shot of British outposts, then fired at any living object they could see. They terrorized the whole British camp. Jugeat's Choctaws also helped keep the British nerves on edge. They patrolled the edge of the swamp, leaping unperceived from one log to another. As they surveyed the enemy they shot every redcoat who came within rifle range. "Not less than fifty British soldiers were killed and many more severely wounded by this method of assassination." [2]

The *Louisiana* dropped down river each day to gall the British and to destroy any emplacements they might have made during the previous night. After Pakenham had complained of "those contemptible militia" mistaking a reconnaissance in force for a real attack, Admiral Cochrane had cryptically retorted: "Now that the infantry has failed to scare the Americans from their line, we must bring more heavy artillery from the ships. If we fail to blast them from behind that ditch, then we must storm their little mud piles." [3]

Gibbs was bitter. "And if the cannon fail," he asked, "how are you going to make regular approaches in this ground where you can't dig more than two feet without making a well of water? How can parallels and zigzags be pushed in such soil?"

Pakenham replied, "The operation can be conducted by saprolling. We will use hogsheads filled with raw cotton for saps." [4]

Gibbs left the council in despair.

So now more cannon were being brought from the fleet. Sailors—Cochrane's tough sailors—rowed boats filled with wounded soldiers sixty miles out to the ships, then rowed back those sixty miles with guns and ammunition. Soldiers manning long dragropes hauled the guns over a road the British had constructed along Bayou Bienvenu. This road through the cypress swamp was soft and miry everywhere and corduroyed where otherwise the swamp would have been impassable.

---

[2] Buell, *History of Jackson*, I, 416.

[3] Adams, *History of United States*, VIII, 357.

[4] Buell, *History of Jackson*, I, 412-13. In this reference Buell quotes from an edition of Gleig which this writer could not secure.

It took three days—the last three days of 1814—to get the additional guns to British headquarters. As those days passed Jackson was apprehensive. What was Pakenham waiting for? Choctaws had thoroughly scouted the north and west shores of Lake Borgne and had found not the slightest sign of activity to indicate an attack by way of Chef Menteur and the Gentilly plain.

Maybe the British would cross the river and attack on the west bank! Jackson sent Latour with 150 Negroes to establish a line behind Morgan's camp. To be effective this line would have to reach from the river to the swamp on the west.

Meanwhile Patterson was busily establishing a marine battery on the levee behind this new line on the west bank of the Mississippi. He took a 24-pounder from the *Louisiana* and on December 30 found that this land gun was more effective than guns on the *Louisiana*. So the next day, December 31, he removed two more guns (12-pounders) from the ship. Then he learned from a deserter that the British were getting hot shot ready to destroy the ship on her next sally. Patterson now sent the *Louisiana* up river out of range but detailed most of her Baratarians to man his land battery.

That night, the last night of the year, sounds of hammering came from the enemy lines. Hinds and his men investigated and reported that the British were erecting batteries within 700 yards of Jackson's line.

The redcoats were building three new batteries and having trouble. Digging for earth they struck water. Under the delusion that sugar would prove as effective as soil in checking the progress of cannon balls, they decided to use the sugar stored in plantation warehouses. Thousands of pounds worth of American sugar went into the British war effort as full hogsheads were rolled into position. While this work was in progress, enough powder and ball for six hours of continuous cannonading were brought to the batteries.[5]

By dawn the British had in place no less than 24 guns and perhaps, as the subaltern says, 30 guns. Battery No. 6 on the levee opposite

---

[5] Gleig, *Campaigns of British Army*, 1833 London Edition, 344; *A Subaltern in America*, 1833 Philadelphia edition, 248.

Patterson's marine battery had two (four?) guns. Battery No. 7 and Battery No. 8 on the levee below Battery No. 6 had seven guns. Three batteries on the plain 700 yards from Jackson's line were No. 5, No. 4 and No. 3. They mounted fifteen guns. Not counting the guns in Battery No. 1 and Battery No. 2 (behind and to the right of No. 5, No. 4 and No. 3), one gets a total of twenty-four (twenty-six?) guns. These would be served by regular artillerists and would throw a greater weight of metal than Jackson's fifteen guns.[6] Three of Jackson's fifteen guns (Patterson's marine battery) were three-quarters of a mile from the main British battery of six 18-pounders. However, Dominique You and Renato Beluche (each now commanding a twenty-four) were directly opposite the six enemy 18-pounders.

---

[6] *Ibid.*, 249.

British guns would throw at least 350 pounds to Jackson's 224. Adams, *History of United States*, VIII, 361-62. On his main line Jackson had seven effective batteries by January 1. They were:

Battery No. 1, 3 guns	seventy feet from the bank of the river, was commanded by Captain Humphreys of the United States Artillery. It consisted of two brass 12-pounders, served by soldiers belonging to the regular artillery; and a 6-inch howitzer on field carriages, served by dragoons of St. Gème's company.
Battery No. 2, 1 gun	ninety yards from No. 1, was a 24-pounder commanded by Lieutenant Norris of the navy and served by part of the Baratarian crew which had manned the *Carolina*.
Battery No. 3, 2 guns	fifty yards from No. 2, contained two 24-pounders. Dominique You and Renato Beluche with their Bartarians manned these guns.
Battery No. 4, 1 gun	twenty yards from No. 3, had a 32-pounder. Lieutenant Crawley of the navy and part of the *Carolina* crew manned this gun.
Battery No. 5, 2 guns	one hundred and ninety yards from No. 4, had two 6-pounders. Colonel Piere and Lieutenant Kerr of the artillery commanded.
Battery No. 6, 1 gun	thirty-six yards from No. 5, was a brass 12-pounder. It was commanded by Garriques Flaujeac—one of the four members of the legislature at the front—and served by a company of Francs under Lieutenant Bertel.

In addition to more guns and a greater weight of metal, the British had another advantage over the Americans. When they were ready they could concentrate their fire on the point or points they chose. Moreover, since Jackson's batteries were on high platforms, they were much easier targets than the low British batteries. With Jackson's guns dismounted, Pakenham's infantry could go through the breach and get behind the American line.

Jackson was prepared for such a contingency. Two miles behind his breastworks he had thrown up a second line on Dupré plantation; and one and a half miles behind this a third line was begun on Montreuil plantation.

Old Hickory was up early on January 1. By the time he had completed his inspection it was daylight. A heavy winter fog made it impossible for him to see more than a few feet in any direction. He knew there could not be any action until the fog lifted. Someone suggested that since it was New Year's Day there should be a parade. Jackson agreed and then went into Macarty mansion to rest a little.

Soon the camp had a festive air as bands tuned up and played " Yankee Doodle " and the " Marseillais." Many visitors arrived from New Orleans to see their relations and friends. They milled around in the field where tents were pitched.

In the opposite camp, a hundred yards or so behind British batteries, lay Pakenham's infantry, anxiously waiting for the sun to rise; and, as the subaltern said, " confidently anticipating that long before his setting, we should be snugly housed in the city of New Orleans. But the sun . . . was slow of making his appearance;

Battery No. 7, one hundred and ninety yards from No. 6, had a long brass 18-pound culverine and a 6-pounder. These were commanded by 2 guns Lieutenant Spotts and Chauveau and served by gunners of the United States Artillery.

Battery No. 8, sixty yards from No. 7 and on the edge of the woods, was a small brass carronade with an imperfect carriage; therefore it was not very effective.

Latour, *Historical Memoir*, 147-48.

a heavy mist obscured him; and the morning was far advanced before it cleared away." [7]

When the fog lifted the American camp was fully exposed to the British. They had heard bands playing and now they could see the different regiments on parade, mounted officers riding backwards and forwards through the ranks, colors floating in the air.

British gunners nearest the river had their batteries ready to fire at Macarty House where they hoped to entomb Jackson and his staff. All the rest had their aim set for the batteries which had destroyed their guns on December 28—the twenty-fours of Dominique and Beluche. That was where the British expected to make a breach through which the infantry would storm. [8]

The instant the signal was given, all the British guns and rocket tubes let go. Their thunderous crash made the delta tremble. A hundred balls, rockets, shells struck Macarty House. Bricks and splinters flew in every direction. One man was knocked down by a flying splinter but no one was hurt.

Jackson and his staff ran for the line. They found Humphrey at Battery No. 1 calmly chewing his cigar. Norris and his Baratarian crew were at No. 2. At No. 3 Dominique was standing on the parapet studying the enemy through a spy glass. A cannon ball whizzed by and scorched his arm. He screamed a curse and shook his fist, crying in French, " I'll make you pay for this! " [9]

Then the little Frenchman calmed himself, gave orders to his crew " to cram their gun to the mouth with terrible chain-shot and ponderous ship cannister, and every description of destructive missile." His shot knocked the biggest British gun to pieces, collapsed the flimsy sugar foundation and killed six men. Beluche fired his twenty-four while Dominique's crew reloaded. These two kept up a steady, alternate fire. [10]

---

[7] 1833 Philadelphia edition, 249.

[8] *Ibid.*; Latour, *Historical Memoir*, 132; Nolte, *Fifty Years in Both Hemispheres*, 218.

[9] *Ibid.*; Walker, *Jackson and New Orleans*, 258.

[10] *Ibid.*; Nolte, *Fifty Years in Both Hemispheres*, 218. Captain R. N. Hill said: " The battery of theirs that did us by far the most damage was the third one from the

Within forty minutes Jackson's batteries dismounted five enemy guns and disabled eight more so that they could not be pointed. With only nine guns left, enemy fire began to slacken. The invaders had a ten minute start in this artillery duel. When they blew up a caisson which contained a hundred pounds of powder, they thought they had made their breach. British troops in the ditches and at the batteries gave three cheers. Then American artillery answered and their shots became more terrible as the British realized too late that they were firing too high and had used up most of their "hardly-collected ammunition." [11] Cannon balls which did hit the soft earth of Jackson's line sank in easily and reinforced the breastwork. One ball struck a cotton bale, set it on fire and knocked it over the embankment. Its smoke blinded the gunners. Some of Plauché's men slid into the ditch and put out the fire.

Meanwhile, Patterson's marine battery silenced enemy guns on the levee.[12] The British infantry never had a chance to get started. In the afternoon Pakenham gave orders to withdraw from the 600-yard line. His men retired baffled and discouraged. That night working parties were sent to retrieve the guns. The subaltern said: "It was my fortune to accompany them. The labour of dragging a number of huge ships' guns out of the soft soil into which they had sunk, crippled, too, as most of them were in their carriages, was more extreme by far than any one expected to find it; indeed, it was not till four o'clock in the morning that our task came to a conclusion, and even then it had been very imperfectly performed." [13]

Pakenham's costly effort had only slightly hurt the Americans. Three of their guns had been damaged, two caissons blown up and

---

right. . . . This battery mounted 24-pounders which were fired alternately with great deliberation and with unvarying effect." Quoted in Buell, *History of Jackson*, I, 419.

[11] Admiral Sir Edward Codrington, quoted in Adams, *History of United States*, VIII, 364.

[12] In reporting this battle, Patterson again did not name a single Baratarian. Instead he made haste to say: "I beg leave particularly to name lt. Campbell, acting sailing-master John Gates, acting midshipman Philip Philibert, of the Louisiana, and sailing-master Haller, of the late schooner Carolina." To Secretary of Navy, Marine batteries five miles below New Orleans, January 2, 1815, Master Commandant's Letters, 1815.

[13] *A Subaltern in America*, 1833 Philadelpia edition, 251.

34 persons killed or wounded. Eleven of these casualties were persons going to or returning from camp.[14] The British loss was greater. Captain Hill said there were 31 killed and 39 wounded, " the great disproportion of killed to wounded being due to the fact that all the hits were by round shot or heavy grape—no small arms being used on either side." [15]

Admiral Cochrane's official report was laconic. It said: " On the 1st instant batteries were opened; but our fire not having the desired effect, the attack was deferred until the arrival of troops under Major-General Lambert." [16]

[14] Latour, *Historical Memoir*, 134-35; Adams, *History of United States*, VIII, 364.

[15] Buell, *History of Jackson*, I, 420. Cooke says the British loss was 142, *Attack on New Orleans*, 212; British return of casualties between the 1st and 5th of January, 1815—76 killed and wounded, 2 missing, James, *Military Occurrences*, II, 543.

[16] Admiral Codrington, quoted in Adams, *History of United States*, VIII, 365.

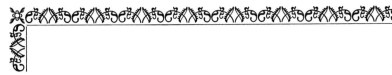

BIVOUAC,

JANUARY 1 TO JANUARY 8

J ACKSON WAITED SEVEN DAYS FOR THE ATTACK OF THE ENEMY.
He was compelled to wait. He could not take the offensive and
destroy or capture the British army because *he did not have enough
guns.*[1]

At the first hint that the British intended to invade Louisiana,
Jackson informed the Secretary of War that he did not have arms
for his volunteers and had suggested that they be sent immediately.
Secretary Monroe then ordered a supply to be shipped from Pittsburgh. But the contractor, instead of shipping the guns on a steam-
boat, sent them on a slow flatboat which stopped on the way to
traffic and trade the different articles with which it was laden.[2]

On January 1, but after the battle of that day, the second division
of Louisiana Militia arrived—500 men from the parishes above
Baton Rouge. They did not have guns.[3] Jackson ordered them to
camp behind Piernas Canal near his second line. The first regiment
of Louisiana Militia was already in position in the wood on the

---

[1] Jackson to Monroe, Camp four miles below New Orleans, January 9, 1815, Bassett
(ed.), *Correspondence*, II, 136-37; Reid and Eaton, *Life of Jackson*, 1817 edition, 272;
Latour, *Historical Memoir*, 142-43; extract of a letter from Claiborne to Eligins Fro-
mentin, Boston *Daily Advertiser*, February 7, 1815.

[2] Reid and Eaton, *Life of Jackson*, 271-72; Monroe to Willie Blount, November 3,
1814, Bassett (ed.), *Correspondence*, II, 85.

[3] Reid and Eaton, *Life of Jackson*, 333.

(119)

banks of this canal. It was important to guard Piernas Canal since it was the only water route by which the enemy could penetrate behind Jackson's main line. Schooners, after ascending Bayou Bienvenu, could come up Piernas Canal.[4]

Major General John Thomas arrived on Wednesday, January 4, with about 2,250 Kentucky Militia. Included in this number were 45 volunteers from Indiana.[5] The northern campaigns had drained Kentucky of firearms, so that two-thirds of the Kentuckians came without any arms, expecting to be supplied in New Orleans.[6]

Jackson was stunned. "I don't believe it," he cried. "I have never in my life seen a Kentuckian without a gun, a pack of cards and a jug of whiskey." [7]

Jackson sent John Adair with 500 of the Kentuckians who had arms to support Carroll on the main line, but there was nothing he could do with the remaining 1,750 except place them with the unarmed Louisiana Militia on his second line and, "by the show they might make, add to his appearance and numbers, without at all increasing his strength." [8]

Several days before this, a search had been made in every house in New Orleans for guns. Only a few ancient Spanish muskets were found. The four companies of old men guarding the city gave up their guns and armed themselves with fowling pieces and pikes, so that 400 more Kentuckians were armed by January 7.[9]

However, Jackson's army behind the mud ramparts of Rodriguez

---

[4] Latour, *Historical Memoid*, 129.

[5] Buell, *History of Jackson*, II, 45.

[6] John Frost, *Pictorial Life of Andrew Jackson* (Philadelphia, 1847), 302; Latour, *Historical Memoir*, 141.

[7] Buell, *History of Jackson*, I, 423.

Not only were the Kentuckians without arms, they were almost naked and half-starved. The people of New Orleans and the river parishes remedied their " deplorable want of clothing in the inclement weather." They contributed $16,000 with which they bought blankets, woolen cloth, and shoes stored in warehouses. The blankets and woolens were distributed among the ladies of New Orleans. Within one week they made 1,200 blanket cloaks, 275 waistcoats, 1,127 pairs of pataloons, and 800 shirts. Latour, *Historical Memoir*, 142.

[8] Reid and Eaton, *Life of Jackson*, 333.

[9] *Niles' Register*, VII (February 11, 1815), 376; Bassett (ed.), *Correspondence*, II, 129 n.; ———, *Life of Jackson*, 190.

Canal was impregnable because the *cannoniers* had plenty of ammunition. Ever since the night battle of December 23, the artillery had annoyed and impeded the enemy. Latour says, and other eyewitnesses agree, that " whenever a group of four or five men showed themselves, they were instantly dispersed by our balls or shells. The advantage we derived from that almost incessant cannonading on both banks of the Mississippi, was that we exercised our gunners, annoyed the enemy to such a degree that he could not work at any fortification, nor indeed come within the reach of our cannon by day, and was deprived of all repose during the night." [10]

An Ordnance Report for October, 1814, says there was in New Orleans at this time

    37 cannon mounted
 3,335 cannon cartridges, filled and empty
56,108 pounds gunpowder
28,746 cannon shot of different sizes
21,867 musket cartridges
12,321 flints

This report was made *after* Patterson's descent on Laffite's establishment at Grande Terre. Since the spring of 1814, the Baratarians had been delivering ammunition to Mexican rebels for New Orleans

---

[10] Latour, *Historical Memoir*, 143.

The French genius of Jackson's *cannoniers* is evident in the names of those who directed the gun crews: Dominique You, Renato Beluche, Garrigues Flaujeac, Bertel, and Chauveau. Jackson's 10-inch mortar was useless until Jules Lefevre, one of Napoleon's eagles and a veteran marine artillerist, took command of it. At some of the batteries, an Anglo-Saxon and a Frenchman commanded, but Jackson's aides usually gave all credit to the Anglo-Saxon, as at Battery No. 7 where Spotts and Chauveau commanded. Reid and Eaton say, for example, that on January 8, " Battery No. 7 was ably served by lieutenant Spotts." This was true, but it was also true that Battery No. 7 was ably served by the Frenchman Chauveau.

A gentleman from New Orleans, writing to a member of Congress, January 13, 1815, said: " Many men distinguished themselves at our batteries whose names until lately were unknown; the privateering class, formerly yclept *Baratarians,* have produced a corps of skillful artillerists. Behind our entrenchments, the discipline of the English troops is not feared, nor our want of it felt; the more regular they are in approaches and attacks, the greater is the loss they sustain, and perhaps the very irregularity of our fire makes it more destructive." *Niles' Register*, VII (February 11, 1815), 375.

[11] George Bomford, Lieutenant Colonel, United States Ordnance to Hon. James Monroe, Secretary of War, Boston *Daily Advertiser*, February 25, 1815.

merchants. The first shipment was 80,000 pounds.[12] Baratarians were skilled in making gunpowder and Laffite had full magazines near New Orleans. Laffite was not bragging when he told Jackson he could furnish ammunition for an army of 30,000.[13]

Because the Baratarians wholeheartedly cooperated in the war effort, Patterson was able not only to keep the *Louisiana* loaded with ammunition to supply his battery on the west bank of the Mississippi; but also, as Claiborne reported to President Madison, Patterson was able to furnish promptly " to the army and militia such supplies of arms and ammunition as could be spared from the naval stores, or prepared by his marines—," which would be the Baratarians.[14]

Apparently Claiborne was not so prompt in forwarding these supplies to Jackson. Nolte says: " The first week of the new year was occupied in strengthening our defences, and it was particularly ordered to have plenty of ammunition in readiness. The munitions were in charge of Gov. Claiborne, who was so frightened that he could scarcely speak. On the first of January ammunition was wanting at batteries Nos. 1 and 2. Jackson sent in fury for Claiborne, who was with the second division, and said to him, ' By the Almighty God, if you do not send me balls and powder instantly, I shall chop off your head, and have it rammed into one of those field-pieces.' "[15]

While Jackson barked at " Clabo," Pakenham was waiting for supplies, guns, and reinforcements. On the first of January he had sent the *Dictator 64* to Havana with about 400 passengers—" soldiers wives, and sick and wounded or disabled soldiers, to relieve the enemy's camp of its ineffectives, and also to obtain provisions for those that remained. The Captain of the *Dictator* immediately contracted for, and began to take on board with all haste 4000 barrels of flour, at 23 dollars *per barrel.*"[16]

---

[12] Faye, " Privateersmen of the Gulf," 22; USDC of La., Case No. 817.

[13] *Journal of Jean Laffite,* 60.

[14] Patterson to Secretary of the Navy, Marine Battery Five Miles below Neworleans [sic], January 13, 1815, Master Commandant's Letters, 1815; Rowland (ed.), *Claiborne Letter Books,* VI, 335.

[15] Nolte, *Fifty Years in Both Hemispheres,* 219.

[16] *Niles' Register,* February 4, 1815, 356; February 11, 1815, 378.

An observer at Havana reported that a brig from New Providence had been permitted to take from the royal arsenal at Havana " 18 pieces of brass cannon for the use of the enemy at New Orleans, and that they were carried thence in the night to save appearances." [17]

Pakenham was waiting also for the arrival of Major General John Lambert with two regiments, the 7th and 43rd, " mustering upwards of seventeen hundred bayonets." The British expetced much from these troops who had not suffered " the galling and unmilitary trials that their fellow soldiers had been put to." After landing, these troops were reviewed with their backs turned towards the enemy's line. Pakenham did not appear at this review because " he was up in a tree in the pine-wood, examining the works of the Americans." [18]

These reinforcements, together with more sailors and marines from the fleet increased Pakenham's force to eight thousand men—" a force which in almost any other quarter of America would have been irresistible." [19] But in Louisiana the flower of the British army had found itself " living targets set up before the elite of the round-hatted Americans." Fatigue, frustration, and hunger were undermining the confidence of those who had pillaged in Spain and France and along the Chesapeake. They no longer had the cocksureness of that Major Mitchell, one of the prisoners taken on the night of December 23, who, when offered clean linen " politely declined it on the ground that his own baggage would be up in a few days." [20] Instead, " some-

---

[17] *Ibid.*

[18] Cooke, *Narrative of Events*, 215-16.
One of the new arrivals was fascinated with the two hundred or so Indians camped at the left of his hut. After describing the men, he said: " The married women or squaws, are in a state of nudity, with the exception of one petticoat reaching to the middle of the calf of the leg; the daughters of twelve years of age are entirely without covering, and squat in the white ashes cross-legged, like their parents; and when they have occasion to move about, the ashes from the fire sticking like feathers to their posteriors, and as dame nature has cast the part in so many moulds, no further description can be requisite to assist the tittering faculties." *Ibid.*, 166.

[19] *A Subaltern in America*, 1826 London edition, 320. The 1836 London edition, page 330, states that the new arrivals increased Pakenham's force to 6,000 men. A collation of the different editions brings out some interesting alibis.

[20] Letter from a gentleman in New Orleans to a member of Congress, *Niles' Register*, VII (February 11, 1815), 375. This same correspondent noted also that " many of the English officers have brought their families with them, and it is said they have a

thing like murmuring began to be heard in the camp." [21] Perhaps
the main reason was that stomachs were empty.

The "long-suffering sailors" had brought guns, ammunition, and
troops from the fleet, but very little food. Officers still had small
rations of salt beef, a few biscuits, and a little rum. Soldiers had less.
Until they learned better, they tried to stave off hunger by eating
raw sugar from hogsheads—"a thick, sticky mass of black stuff,
full of grit and little splinters of cane; having a sickish flavor and
leaving a bad taste in the mouth, besides producing nausea or
diarrhaea (*sic*) if taken in any quantity." [22]

The men in Jackson's camp were well-fed. New Orleans was full
of flour, corn meal, meat which had not been exported because of
the blockade and which continued to come from up river. Jackson
had impresssed every horse, mule, and wagon for transport service.
These brought a daily supply of cornbread, sweet potatoes, bacon,
and other food from the city. Creoles drank coffee while westerners
drank whiskey.

Letters written in Jackson's camp show a different spirit from the
memoirs written by Pakenham's subalterns. Instead of complaining,
as did the British, about not being able to sleep because of the continuous shower of cannon balls, a militiaman in Jackson's camp
wrote on the day before the final battle:

> We have become so used to the sound of cannon within these two weeks
> past that no one appears to attach any importance to it, and even women
> who never heard of a camp before, will enter it in the heat of battle with-
> out fear. I think now, all I have read of wars and battles is mere stuff—
> that its terrors are more horrid in imagination than in reality. Some of
> the most cowardly fellows are among our first rate warriors . . . but practice
> makes everything familiar to the human mind, and I do really believe that
> our troops are now so familiarized to scenes of blood, that they would
> not hesitate, if commanded, to march in column up to the mouth of a
> cannon. I cannot conceive how the men at Washington allowed the same
> cowardly Englishmen to alarm them when they attacked at Bladensburg. . . .

collector aboard. Everything proclaims their intention of a permanent establishment
and their confidence of ultimate success."

[21] *A Subaltern in America*, 1826 London edition, 318.

[22] Cited from account of R. N. Hill in Buell, *History of Jackson*, I, 420.

You will laugh at my calling the British soldiers cowardly. I don't know if the epithet may be applicable to the whole army, but to the divisions we have seen it appertains with great justice. On the first assault the enemy made upon our entrenchments, on the 28th ult., they came in three columns, first on the right, second to the center, and third to the extreme left. They marched up in solid mass, until they came within about 400 yards, they then halted and displayed; we then saluted them with grape and cannister shot; they immediately formed solid column again, but with all the thrashing that the officers could give them, not a man would advance another inch—in this situation they stood until we gave them another round of cannister and grape, when down they fell upon their bellies and laid there until dark, and then sneaked off under cover of night.[23]

If any of Jackson's troops had cause to complain, it was Coffee's Tennesseans. From the 24th of December until the 20th of January they worked and slept in mud, and never showed the least symptoms of discontent or impatience. Jackson's ramparts on Rodriguez Canal stretched in a fairly straight line *on firm ground* from the river to fifty yards beyond Battery No. 8—a distance of about 700 yards. Fifty yards beyond Battery No. 8 the line was not visible to the enemy because it plunged into the woods for 750 yards, still in a fairly straight line. Then, because the land inclined away from the river, the woods became impassable. Enormous holes full of water from the canal made it necessary to turn the line at a 90 degree angle and bend it back 200 yards. Coffee's Tennesseans guarded the 750-yard sector in the woods and the 200-yard end. To do so they had to camp there. The ground was so low and difficult to drain that the Tennesseans literally lived in water, walking knee deep in mud. Several tents were pitched on small isles surrounded with mud or water. The 200-yard end had to be guarded constantly for the enemy, under cover of bushes, might otherwise get behind Jackson's line.[24]

Jackson was anxious about possible British penetration from that end back to Piernas Canal; so on January 3, he sent Reuben Kemper

---

[23] Letter dated January 7, 1815, *Niles' Register*, VII (February 11, 1815), 377-78.
[24] Latour, *Historical Memoir*, 149-50.

from Feliciana (parish above Baton Rouge) and eleven Louisiana volunteers on a scouting expedition. They descended Piernas Canal in boats to Bayou Bienvenu and proceeded down that bayou to its junction with Bayou Manzant. They stopped occasionally and climbed trees to see whether or not they could locate the British. They had almost reached Bayou Manzant before they discovered the fortified enclosure Pakenham's troops had built at its junction with Bienvenu. Kemper left five men to guard his boats while he and the rest went to reconnoiter from the prairie. They had gone about half a mile when they saw the enemy coming up the bayou in five vessels. They saw sailors looking out from the mast head and when the vessels got near Kemper's boats, the British fired on them. Four of Kemper's men escaped but one was taken prisoner.

The British set fire to the prairie as they went on up the bayou " so that whoever happened to be in it had to run from the flames rapidly gaining on the grass . . . which was . . . as thick as wheat in a field." Kemper and his men worked their way toward Villeré's Canal. Where it enters Manzant, they discovered a strong force behind breastworks guarding magazines. Kemper and his scouts were back in camp by January 5.[25] Only men like Kemper and his Louisianians could have found their way through the swamps and trembling prairies and circle back with precise reports to Jackson in less than two days.

Jackson and his troops were able to see some actvity in front of them. After the battle on New Year's Day they saw the British working on a large quadrilateral redoubt. Its interior dimensions were 80 feet × 62 feet × 108 feet × 70 feet. It was located near the woods on Bienvenu plantation. Jackson's heavy pieces of artillery did not cease firing on the working parties, but they made some progress because the officer commanding them stood upon the parapet; and as soon as he saw the fire of Jackson's guns, he gave a signal to his men who instantly flattened behind the parapet.[26]

British workmen also were constantly galled as they built a square redoubt at the ditch separating Bienvenu and Chalmette plantations.

---

[25] *Ibid.*, 138-40.　　　　　　　　　　[26] *Ibid.*, 136.

This redoubt was in front of Jackson's Battery No. 7. Not until the night of January 7, Saturday night, did Pakenham re-establish the batteries that had been destroyed the previous Sunday, the batteries on Chalmette plantation. Shortly after nightfall hammer strokes of the Brtish resounded even within the American lines and gave a " note of preparation." Jackson's outposts reported this activity and also that British guards had been reinforced.

Meanwhile from other sources Jackson knew the British were about to attack on both sides of the Mississippi. A brig from Jamaica had been captured near Chef Menteur. It was loaded with rum, bread, and munitions. Ten prisoners from this brig told Jackson of the arrival of Lambert with reinforcements. Deserters from the British camp confirmed this report and added that a water passage was being dug to the Mississippi. All week long the British made Negroes of the planatations in their possession cut through the levee and continue Villeré's Canal until by Saturday it connected with the river.

On that day there was a great deal of activity in front of the British camp but the distance was so great that Americans could not see distinctly what the enemy was doing. Jackson took his old telescope to the second story of Macarty House and was able to see that on Laronde's (three plantations away) soldiers were making fascines and ladders. Beyond that on Lacoste's and Villeré's plantations troops continually marched and maneuvered so that they concealed operations behind them. Jackson sent word to Patterson to go down his side of the river and look across at the British.

Patterson and Morgan were responsible for the defense of the west bank. Immediately after the battle of New Year's Day, Jackson had sent his chief engineer, Latour, across the river to assist Morgan in choosing an advanced position for a line of defense. Latour surveyed the situation and chose a place where the distance between the river and the impassable woods was only 900 yards wide. Several cannon and 500 men behind breastworks here could hold the line. It could not be turned because to attack the line the enemy would have to advance on the open plain.[27]

---

[27] *Ibid.*, 166-68.

When Latour went to advise Morgan he found Patterson with him. Patterson's batteries (three twenty-fours and six twelves) were strung out for a mile along the river edge. Some were below Latour's projected line. Patterson's guns were placed to enfilade Pakenham's troops if they came up the levee or the plain on Jackson's side of the river. It seems as though Patterson wanted to be sure that he played with the big boys. His guns were not in position to cover his own bank against attack from below.[28]

Morgan rejected Latour's proposed 900-yard line and chose a line 2000 yards long (longer than Jackson's line on Rodriguez Canal which from the river to the woods was 700 yards and on which there were eight batteries) below Patterson's batteries along the shallow Raguet Canal. This selection was made early in the week, probably on Monday. By Saturday 200 yards of breastworks had been thrown up beginning at the river. These were protected by one 12-pounder and two 6-pounders. Behind these breastworks were Morgan and 500 Louisiana militia. Nine-tenths of the line (1800 yards) had no protection except a shallow ditch.

This was the situation on Saturday afternoon, January 7, when Patterson dropped down river to see what the British were doing. He looked across and still was not much concerned about his own side of the river. He reported to Jackson saying, " The British have dug out Villeré's Canal to the River, and from the number of men, soldiers and seamen, I apprehend they will get their Boats into the River tonight." In another note he added: " Be assured that no exertion on my part shall be wanting to defeat the attempts of the Enemy, but we are extremely weak on this side, require a strong reinforcement. . . . I consider the firing of the Enemy this evening, as a feint to draw your attention from their operations below, which I apprehend they will carry into execution to-night; but I hope and trust they will meet defeat. Come when they may, my Guns shall roar long and loud depend upon it! " [29]

---

[28] Adams, *History of United States*, VIII, 370; M'Afee, *History of the Late War*, 519-20; Bassett, *Life of Jackson*, 198-99.
[29] West bank of Mississippi, January 7, 1815, Bassett (ed.), *Correspondence*, II, 132.

Jackson paid some attention to Patterson's plea. He ordered Adair to send 400 Kentucky militia to reinforce Morgan's camp. This order Adair gave to Colonel Davis at 7 P. M. Colonel Davis immediately marched 400 men to New Orleans—about five miles. There 170 of them were armed. Some of the muskets had no flints. Those who had such guns would have to substitute pebbles. The unarmed Kentuckians returned to camp below New Orleans.[30]

Colonel Davis and his 170 armed men were ferried across the river; then they marched five more miles over bad roads, sometimes knee-deep in mud, and reached Morgan's camp at 4 A. M. General Morgan was glad to see them. Keeping his Louisiana Militia behind the line, he immediately sent the Kentuckians a half mile down the river beyond the breastworks to meet the enemy.

Meanwhile, in the British camp, a soldier who had escaped from Jackson's line on the night of January 6 told Pakenham about the unarmed condition of many of Jackson's troops; and, " pointing to the centre of general Carroll's division, as a place occupied by militia alone, recommended it as the point where an attack might be most safely made." [31]

The next day, Saturday, January 7, Pakenham called his last council of war. Admiral Cochrane was there. He was the one who had suggested that Pakenham send enough troops across the river to seize Patterson's guns and turn them on Jackson's army while the main British force stormed the American line.[32] Admiral Malcolm was also present, the same who had held a ball on his flagship, the *Royal Oak*, as the fleet crossed the Atlantic; and who " with the honourable Mrs. Mullens " had opened the ball with a country dance.[33]

---

[30] John Adair to Governor Isaac Shelby, New Orleans, March 20, 1815, *Niles' Register*, VIII (April 29, 1815), 157; Latour, *Historical Memoir*, 170; Bassett, *Life of Jackson*, 197-98; Adams, *History of United States*, VIII, 370-71.

[31] Reid and Eaton, *Life of Jackson*, 334-35; S. Putnam Waldo (ed.), *Memoirs of Andrew Jackson* (Hartford, 1819), 244; Colyar, *Life and Times of Jackson*, I, 335.

[32] Adams, *History of United States*, VIII, 367.

[33] *A Subaltern in America*, 1826 London edition, 65. " Mrs. Mullens, an elegant lady then in the fleet, had come over to grace the fashionable circles of New Orleans. She

Pakenham and his generals and admirals reviewed the strategy of their simultaneous attack on both sides of the river which was to take place two hours before dawn the next day while it was still dark enough to conceal their movements. Major General Gibbs with 2,200 men would lead the main attack against Carroll's center which was behind Batteries No. 7 and No. 8. (These batteries the English did not fear.)

Major General Keane would lead 1,200 troops in a sham attack to the right along the river. This column would draw the fire of Jackson's heavy batteries (Nos. 1, 2, 3 and 4) until Gibbs could break through at Battery No. 7.[34] There were no cannon on the 750 yards of Jackson's line in the cypress woods. Gibb's column could approach Battery No. 7 under cover of those woods to within 200 yards of the Americans. A regiment of West Indian Negroes would support Gibbs's right. They would advance through the woods and distract Coffee and Jugeat's Choctaws so that they would not go to the aid of Carroll.

Major General Lambert with 1,400 reserves would be in the rear center. Thus 5,300 men would be ready to assault Jackson's line while Colonel Thornton with 1,400 men across the river captured Patterson's guns and turned them on Jackson's west flank. Seamen and troops detailed for other duties swelled the total of the attacking force to about 8,000.[35]

Pakenham appointed the 44th to lead Gibbs's column. These 400 men were to advance over broken ground and unseen obstacles lugging fascines (made of ripe sugar cane and therefore heavy) and ladders ten feet long so that troops behind them could cross Jackson's

---

had been the life of the squadron, contributing by her fascinating manners and vivacity, to brighten many of the dull and gloomy hours of the long voyage. But her husband was far from being the soul of the army. Son of a lord, he had obtained his promotion more by influence than merit. . . . He had received one honorable wound at Albuera, and that sufficed to fill the measure of his ambition." Walker, *Jackson and New Orleans*, 323.

[34] Gleig, *Campaigns of British Army*, 1836 London edition, 331.
[35] Adams, *History of United States*, VIII, 373; Bassett, *Life of Jackson*, 192-93.

ditch and scale his slippery mud wall. Lieutenant Colonel Mullens (he was only a captain in the regiment) commanded the 44th.

Captain Hill was sent before sunset to instruct the " Honorable Colonel Mullins (*sic*) of the 44th, respecting the redoubt in which the fascines, etc were placed," and to report the result of his interview. Hill found Mullens, read the directions from headquarters to him, and then asked, "Do you thoroughly understand the instructions?"

Mullens replied, "Nothing could be clearer." A little later he cried out, " My regiment has been ordered to execution. Their dead bodies are to be used as a bridge for the rest of the army to march over!" [36]

This cry sounds as though Mullens thought he was to be another Uriah the Hittite whom the captain of the armies had sent to sure death at the front so that King David could have Bathsheba, the wife of Uriah the Hittite. That night, as Mullens led the 44th to the front, he halted for ten minutes at the redoubt where the fascines and ladders were scattered about; but no engineer officer came to point out the equipment. A commanding officer even of a regiment is only a secondary person to the engineer department on such occasions. Mullens passed on and stationed his troops in the lead position without any fascines or ladders.[37]

During the night the rest of the troops moved forward and Pakenham's engineers placed six 18-pounders in position about 700 yards from the Americans to cover the British attack.[38] Jackson's outposts observed and silently moved back as the enemy advanced. In his camp "all was composure," except that Jackson was uneasy about the half-moon shaped redoubt on the river in front of his line. Two of his officers had insisted on Thursday (January 5) that this

---

[36] William James, *Military Occurrences*, II, 374-80 (this account is based on the court maritial of Mullens) ; *A Subaltern in America*, 1826 London edition, 371 ; Parton, *Life of Jackson*, II, 185, 191 (this account quotes Captain Hill) ; Buell, *History of Jackson*, II, 3.

[37] Cooke, *Narrative of Attack*, 247-48.

[38] *Ibid.*, 224-25 ; Adams, *History of United States*, VIII, 372.

bastion for two 6-pounders should be established there to rake a charging column coming up the river road since Battery No. 1 was 70 feet from the Mississippi.[39]

The troops behind Jackson's guns from the redoubt to Battery No. 6 were the 7th regiment next the river, then Beale's Rifles, Plauché's battalion of volunteer uniform companies, Major Lacoste's battalion of Louisiana men of color, Major Daquin's battalion of Haitian men of color, and the 44th. All these corps—from the 7th on the river to the 44th beyond Battery No. 5—were under the command of Colonel Ross and numbered about 1,300 men.

Carroll's 1,400 Tennesseans, supported in their rear by Adair with 520 Kentuckians, were behind Batteries No. 6 and No. 7. To the right of No. 7 were 50 marines under the command of Lieutenant Bellevue. Carroll's command extended fifty yards beyond Battery No. 8 at which point the line entered the woods. Coffee's brigade and Jugeat's Choctaws, about 800 men, were in the woods.

The troops defending Jackson's line totalled approximately 4,000. Behind the line were four small cavalry groups and a strong row of sentries. Along the edge of the woods were some Louisiana Militia.

Jackson started to survey his line shortly after one o'clock on Sunday morning. He began at the right on the river. His face clouded as he looked at the unfinished redoubt 30 yards in front of his line. "I don't like that redoubt. I didn't want it in the first place," he growled, "but my young officers talked me into it."

His spirits lifted when he saw Beale's Rifles and a company of the 7th Infantry ready to defend the redoubt. Battery No. 1 was in good shape. There was Colonel Humphrey with his cigar and St. Gème without his plumed cap. His dragoons and the rest of the 7th were behind the battery. Lieutenant Norris of the navy and Baratarians from the *Carolina* had Battery No. 2 well in hand.

Jackson sniffed. A delicious aroma was coming from Battery No. 3. The Baratarians were making coffee. Odd what a ritual those Frenchmen observed in making coffee. They had to have a

---

[39] Latour, *Historical Memoir*, 144-45; Bassett, *Life of Jackson*, 190.

special drip pot of tin-coated iron. This was placed in a kettle of simmering water so the pot and contents would keep hot but would not boil. A spoonful of the hot water was carefully ladled on the coffee. It must not channel through the grounds but soak them evenly. The first little bit of water barely moistened the coffee. Then a second spoonful of water was added and allowed to drip before the next was added, and the next and the next. It seemed to take a Frenchman hours to make a pot of coffee.

As Jackson approached Dominique You he said. " That smells like better coffee than we can get. Where did you get such fine coffee? " Then he suggested slyly, " Maybe you smuggled it in? "

" Mebbe so, général," grinned Dominique as he handed Jackson a small tin cup full.

Jackson drank the coffee with gusto, thanked the Baratarians, and moved on to complete his inspection. Later, when he again saw Dominique and his battery in action—as he had on December 28th and on New Year's Day, Jackson said to his aides, " If I were ordered to storm the gates of hell, with Captain Dominique as my lieutenant, I would have no misgivings of the result." [40]

---

[40] Saxon, *Laffite the Pirate*, 181.

THE BATTLE

OF THE 8th OF JANUARY

A LITTLE BEFORE DAYBREAK JACKSON'S OUTPOSTS CAME IN without any noise and reported the enemy moving forward in great force. The whole line was tense, expectant. In a few moments there was light, but a heavy mist reduced visibility to 200 yards. The Americans could not see 50 armed boats crossing the river below them.

Those boats were supposed to have reached the west side at midnight, but the banks of the newly dug canal had caved in and choked the channel. The boats had to be dragged through mud. Six hours behind schedule, Thornton, with only 340 troops and 100 seamen and marines (instead of a total of 1,400 men), moved across the river. His seamen rowed in silence with oars muffled and, thanks to the mist, gained the opposite bank without having been perceived. However, the current of the Mississippi had dragged them downstream so that Thornton landed five miles below Patterson's guns which were to be fired on Jackson's line as the starting signal for the battle.

At daybreak Pakenham, mounted on horseback, was on the levee in a central position where he could listen for Thornton's shots and direct the main attack. The mist was the luckiest screen possible, for otherwise the Americans would have seen and opened fire on the boats and on the columns formed only 400 yards in front of Jackson's line.

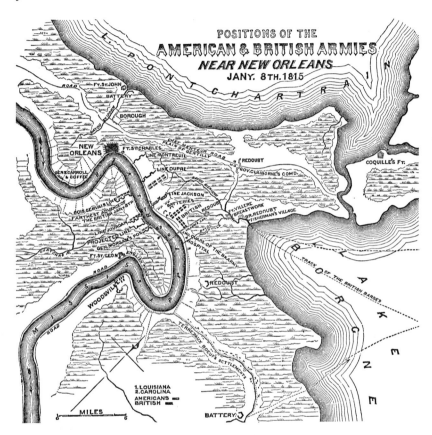

Then the mist began to clear. No sound came from across the river. Pakenham galloped toward his lines. He saw his troops in battle array but not a ladder nor a fascine was upon the field. Gibbs rushed up and cried, " If I live till tomorrow, I'll hang Mullens on the highest tree in the cypress swamp." [1]

Pakenham ordered Mullens to take 300 men and rush back to

---

[1] Colyar, *Life and Times of Jackson*, I, 344; *Niles' Register*, VIII (April 22, 1815), 133.

the redoubts—nearly a quarter of a mile—for fascines and ladders. Breathless with running, only half of them had returned and regained their position when Pakenham gave the signal for attack. Mullens was not one of those who returned. Historians say he was incompetent; but according to his lights he was using common sense.

Confused, many of the 44th threw down their burdens and began to fire. Gibbs's men fired too—they forgot that they were to rush Jackson's line with bayonets. Gibbs rallied his troops. At that instant Jackson's gunners at Battery No. 6 perceived the enemy column moving in formation sixty abreast. They fired their 12-pounder.

Gibbs's troops gave three cheers and charged. Jackson yelled to his men, "Give it to them boys, let's finish this business today!"[2]

Instantly Jackson's whole line was ablaze with cannon fire. Grape shot and cannister ploughed through Gibbs's column. On it came. In a moment it was within easy musket range. Carroll's men fired— a constant rolling fire. The echo from the cannonade and musketry was so tremendous in the forests, "that the vibration seemed as if the earth was cracking and tumbling to pieces, or as if the heavens were rent asunder by the most terrific peals of thunder that ever rumbled; it was the most awful and the grandest mixture of sounds. . . the woods seemed to crack to an interminable distance, each cannon report was answered one hundred fold, and produced an intermingled roar surpassing strange. . . . The flashes of fire looked as if coming out of the bowels of the earth. . . . The reverberation was so intense towards the great wood, that any one would have thought the fighting was going on there."[3]

Gibbs's column recoiled, fled to the woods, to the ditch from which it had started. A captain on the 700 yard line saw "the dark shadows of men, like skirmishers, breaking out the clouds of smoke which slowly and majestically rolled along the surface of the field."

---

[2] *Niles' Register*, VII (February 11, 1815), 376; Washington *National Intelligencer*, February 6, 1815.

[3] Cooke, *Narrative of Attack*, 234-35.

He was so astonished at the panic he saw that he asked a retiring soldier, " Have we or the Americans attacked? " [4]

Gibbs shouted to the 44th. They did not heed but continued their retreat. He galloped a short distance to Pakenham in the rear and cried, " The troops will not obey me! " [5]

Pakenham rode to the 44th and yelled for Mullens but that officer was not to be found. The commander in chief took Mullens' place—dashed to the head of the column and moved it forward 30 or 40 yards. Then a musket shot wounded his knee and killed his horse. Pakenham jumped on another and almost instantly grape shot from Battery No. 8 mortally wounded him.[6]

Gibbs tried to rally the column as the dying Pakenham was carried to the rear. His command was annihilated and 20 yards in front of Jackson's ditch, Gibbs was mortally wounded. A few men did cross the ditch and climb the slippery parapet only to be killed or captured.

Meanwhile, Keane's column had advanced between the river and the levee. Patterson's battery across the river enfiladed the column and killed most of the advance, but Colonel Rennie, leading the remnant, stormed Jackson's unfinished redoubt. Rennie was crawling toward Battery No. 1 when one of Beale's Rifles shot him. He and his followers died in the redoubt.

Keane had held most of his men back. He was watching Gibbs. When he saw confusion in the main attack, Keane obliqued across the field to the rescue. He was wounded and carried from the field as his men fell to the ground.

Within 25 minutes after the battle had started, the three main British commanders were carried off the field and Chalmette plantation was covered with dead and wounded redcoats. Lambert was

---

[4] *Ibid.*, 235.
[5] Bassett, *Life of Jackson*, 194.
[6] *Ibid.*, 195. " The death of the general was a fortunate event for the British. His character was irretrievably ruined if he did not take New Orleans or perish in the attempt . . . the opinion of a British officer taken on the 8th of January." *Niles' Register*, VIII (April 22, 1815), 133.

now commander in chief. He tried to make his 1,400 reserves attack but he could not. So he ordered retreat.

Jackson's musketry blazed away until 8:30. His cannonade did not stop until two in the afternoon.[7] Then the roar of artillery gave place to the most profound silence.

Thornton's attack on the west side of the Mississippi did not get started until musketry fire had ceased on Jackson's line. Then the Americans heard Thornton's guns and looked across the river. They saw the flotilla of enemy boats carrying carronades and cannon, keeping close to the bank and firing on the Kentucky Militia while Thornton's troops on shore drove them back. The Kentuckians returned the fire as they retreated to Morgan's line. There they were given a 300-yard sector of the unfinished 1,800 yards to protect. Thornton's redcoats steadily charged in two columns. One of these moved toward the woods and turned the right of the Kentuckians. Patterson could not fire on the redcoats without killing his own men. With no protection and muskets that were not much good, outflanked on the right and cannonaded with grape-shot on the left, the Kentuckians fled from the points of enemy bayonets. This left the Louisiana Militia exposed. They fled. Patterson spiked his cannon and threw his ammunition in the river.

Thornton chased the Americans until he held the west bank for a mile above Jackson's line. Then he received an order from Lambert to bring his men back across the river.

---

[7] Cooke described the hours during which Jackson's cannoneers plied him and his men with grape and round shot. He says: " Some of the wounded managed to crawl away; but every now and then some unfortunate man was lifted off the ground by round shot, and lay killed or mangled. . . . A wounded soldier, who was lying amongst the slain two hundred yards behind us, continued without any cessation, for two hours, to raise his arm up and down with a convulsive motion, which excited the most painful sensations amongst us; and as the enemy's balls every now and then killed or maimed some soldiers, we could not help casting our eyes toward the moving arm, which really was a *dreadful magnet* of attraction. . . . A tree, about two feet in diameter and fifteen in height, with a few scattered branches at the top, was the only object to break the monotonous scene. . . . The Americans, seeing some persons clustering around it, fired a thirty-two pound shot, which struck the tree exactly in the centre, and buried itself in the trunk with a loud concussion. Curiosity prompted some of us to take a hasty inspection of it, and I could clearly see the rusty ball within the tree." *Narrative of Attack*, 240-41.

In the afternoon Lambert sent a flag of truce to ask permission to bury his dead. Jackson granted a suspension of arms for only two hours. This was wise because the British had command of the west bank, 50 boats in the Mississippi, a blockade at the mouth of the river, and they were approaching Fort St. Philip (50 miles above the mouth of the Mississippi) with two bomb vessels, one sloop, one brig, and one schooner.[8]

A truce line was agreed upon, 300 yards from Jackson's breastworks. No British soldier was to come over this line. Jackson detailed men to help the British gather up their killed and wounded.[9] There were 1,971. The Americans had six killed and seven wounded.[10]

The English buried their dead on a section of Bienvenu plantation. Some of the officers were buried in Villeré's garden. The remains of Pakenham and Gibbs were disembowled and put in casks of rum to be sent to England. About three hundred of the wounded were carried into the American camp. Then they were taken to New Orleans and lodged in the barracks. Captain De Bruys, commander of the city, " represented to the citizens the wants of those unfortunate victims of British ambition, and immediately one hundred and forty matresses, a great number of pillows, with a large quantity of lint and old linen for dressing their wounds, were procured by contributions from all quarters, at a moment when such

---

[8] On the 9th, the enemy opened fire on Fort St. Philip which they continued without much intermission until the morning of the 18th when they withdrew.

[9] As he was helping to gather up the wounded, a Tennessean looked at the long corpse of an Englishman and saw that two bullets had gone through his head. One had struck him over the left eye and passed out back of the right ear. The other hit him between the right nostril and the eye and had come out through the left ear. Either wound must have been instantly fatal. "A little lead wasted there," said the Tennessean. Buell, *History of Jackson*, II, 34-35.

[10] Bassett, *Life of Jackson*, 197. Most of the newspaper accounts say there were between two and three thousand British casualties. Total British casualties since the night of December 23 were 3,326. Total American casualties were one-tenth that number. Latour, *Historical Memoir*, Appendix No. XXIX, lii-liv; Buell, *History of Jackson*, II, 41; Bassett (ed.), *Correspondence*, II, 136-38; *Niles' Register*, VII (February 18, 1815), 386.

articles were extremely scarce in New Orleans, where not a truss of straw could be purchased." [11]

During the next ten days Jackson's artillery annoyed the enemy. Major Hinds wanted to attack with his cavalry; but after consulting with Adair and Coffee, Jackson decided against such a maneuver for Adair had said: " My troops will fight when behind breastworks or in the woods, but do not hazard an attack with raw militia in the open plain." [12]

The British army seemed to be inactive but it was not. Lambert's engineers were building a road to the lake over which the army could withdraw since there were not enough boats to carry off the troops in a body. It took nine days of hard, unceasing labor to construct the semblance of a road. The route was along the margin of the bayous, but there was little room for firm footing. Reeds, cane, and boughs of trees were laid across deep mud holes.

Trimming their fires on the evening of January 18, " and arranging all things in the same order as if no change were to take place, regiment after regiment stole away, as soon as darkness concealed their motions; leaving the piquets to follow as a rear-guard, but with strict injunctions not to retire until daylight began to appear. As may be supposed, the most profound silence was maintained; not a man opening his mouth, except to issue necessary orders, and even then speaking in a whisper." [13]

While the soldiers were still on firm ground the retreat was easy, but as they entered the trembling prairies their troubles began. The first corps beat the flimsy path to pieces. Those who followed floundered along the best they could where the path had been. Not only were the reeds torn asunder and sunk by the pressure of those who had gone before, but the mud had been so churned that at every step soldiers sank to their knees. The night was dark, there was no moon, and it was difficult to follow the soldier ahead.

When one cried, " Help! Help! " a lieutenant started to the rescue

---

[11] Latour, *Historical Memoir*, 177.
[12] Bassett, *Life of Jackson*, 203.
[13] Gleig, *Campaigns of British Army*, 1836 London edition, 349-50.

but he too began to sink in mud up to his breast. He felt himself being smothered but managed a feeble cry of " Help! " Someone threw him a leather canteen strap and dragged him out just as the man he had tried to save sank from view.[14]

Mud was not the only terror. Alligators who inhabited that mud resented the intrusion of these humans. They made the night hideous for the British and obsessed them during the day.

On the morning of the nineteenth a British surgeon came to Jackson and gave him a letter from General Lambert. It announced that the British had left, but that there were eighty soldiers who were too badly wounded to be moved. Would General Jackson please look after them?

Jackson immediately dispatched Dr. David C. Kerr, his surgeon general, with helpers to take care of the eighty; and then with his aides rode to the deserted camp. He saw cannon, thousands of cannon balls, and the public and private possessions left behind by the departing British—mute testimony of the complete victory of his little army.

---

[14] *Ibid.*, 351-52.

TRIUMPH AND TRIAL

The British had covered their dead with Louisiana soil but rains soon caused bodies to rise toward the surface. Legs, arms and heads appeared in many places above ground. The effluvia was insupportable. Jackson decided to move the main part of his army to New Orleans, so on Saturday, January 21, his troops were drawn up behind their ditch ready to march as soon as General Orders were read. Their hearts stirred within them as they listened to these words from their chief:

> The enemy has retreated, and your general has now leisure to proclaim to the world what he has noticed with admiration and pride—your undaunted courage, your patriotism and patience, under hardships and fatigues. Natives of different states, acting together for the first time in this camp, differing in habits and language, instead of viewing in these circumstances the germs of distrust and division, you have made them the source of an honourable emulation. . . . This day completes the fourth week since fifteen hundred of you attacked treble your number of men, who had boasted of their discipline, and their services under a celebrated leader . . . attacked them in their camp, the moment they had profaned the soil of freedom with their hostile tread, and inflicted a blow which was a prelude to the final result of their attempt to conquer, or their poor contrivances to divide us. . . .
>
> Let us be grateful to the God of battles who has directed the arrows of indignation against our invaders, while he covered with his protecting

shield the brave defenders of their country. . . . The consequences of this short but decisive campaign are incalculably important. The pride of our arrogant enemy humbled, his forces broken, his leaders killed, his insolent hopes of our disunion frustrated—his expectation of rioting in our spoils and wasting our country changed into ignominious defeat, shameful flight, and a reluctant acknowledgment of the humanity and kindness of those whom he had doomed to all the horrors and humiliation of a conquered state. . . .

Then Jackson praised every corps: the regulars, Coffee's Tennesseans, Hinds and his Mississippi cavalry, the Kentucky Militia, Jugeat and his Choctaws, the Louisiana Militia, the two corps of colored volunteers, distinguished foreigners, and the Baratarians. Of these last he said:

They performed their duty with zeal and bravery. . . . Captains Dominique and Belluche, lately commanding privateers at Barataria, with part of their former crew and many brave citizens of New Orleans, were stationed at Nos. 3 and 4. The general cannot avoid giving his warm approbation of the manner in which these gentlemen have uniformly conducted themselves while under his command, and of the gallantry with which they have redeemed the pledge they gave at the opening of the campaign to defend the country. The brothers Laffite have exhibited the same courage and fidelity; and the general promises that the government shall be duly apprized of their conduct.[1]

As the troops marched toward the city that clear, cool Saturday morning, Nature seemed to smile upon the heroes who had fought and conquered to save their country. The aged, the infirm, women, children—all went out to meet the men. " The scene was splendid and delightful—it was perhaps the most unmixed triumph that ever occurred on this globe; so few men had fallen in the contest that private regret did not impair public joy. Every eye beamed, every heart beat high. Parents and children, husbands and wives, brothers and sisters were again united, rendered dearer to each other by the peril and danger past." [2]

---

[1] Latour, *Historical Memoir*, Appendix No. LXIX, clxxxii-clxxxvii.
[2] Letter dated New Orleans, January 21, 1815, in Boston *Daily Advertiser*, February 24, 1815.

THE OLD SPANISH CATHEDRAL AND GOVERNMENT HOUSE.

Two days before the return of the army to the city, Jackson had written Father Dubourg requesting that a service of public thanksgiving be performed in the Cathedral. This could not be done immediately on the return of the troops to the city because "the first display was too wild to be controlled by any regular method or system," and because the ladies needed more time to complete their arrangements for a ceremony "sprung from female gratitude and arranged entirely by the ladies." [3]

On the morning of January 23, all was ready and New Orleans was awakened by salvos of artillery. Soon the streets were filled with people on their way to witness the pageantry of Jackson's entrance into the Cathedral.

In the middle of the Place d'Armes and facing the main door of the Cathedral was an arch of triumph with six Corinthian columns, all twined with laurel. From either side of the arch, laurel festoons supported by eighteen pillars (nine on each side) formed an aisle through which General Jackson would walk. On each pillar was a

[3] *Niles' Register*, VIII (May 6, 1815), 163.

medallion with the name of a state surrounded by wreaths of various hues. In front of each pillar stood a young girl in white with a lace veil on her head, " tastefully confined by a white satin bandeau, finished on the left by a golden star." On her left hand she carried a white basket with blue ribbon ornaments and filled with artificial flowers.

Two little girls, each standing on a pedestal, were to suspend a laurel wreath over Jackson's head as he passed under the arch. Near each child was another little girl. One represented Liberty and the other Justice.

Mothers stood behind their daughters (" the states "), and a short distance back of these matrons several very handsome uniform companies were drawn up to keep the people from " incommoding " those taking part in the ceremony. A full band of military music announced the approach of the beloved general, followed by his staff officers. They entered the square by the river gate and when Jackson was under the arch " the little girls managed their wreath to admiration." Miss Louisiana, Dr. Kerr's eight-year-old daughter, stepped forward and presented an address handsomely ornamented, the composition of Mrs. Ellery.[4] Jackson deposited this document in his bosom and then flowers were strewn in his path as he walked down the aisle, bowing to " the states." These fell in line behind him and then their mothers joined the procession.

Father Dubourg, attended by priests, met Jackson at the entrance to the Cathedral and entreated him to remember that his splendid achievements were to be ascribed to Him, to whom all praise is due. " Let the infatuated votary of blind chance," said the prelate, " deride our credulous simplicity; let the cold hearted atheist look for the explanation of such important events to the mere concatenation of human causes; to us, the whole universe is loud in proclaiming a Supreme Ruler who, as he holds the hearts of men, holds also the thread of all contingent occurrences. Whatever be his intermediate agents, still on the secret orders of His all-ruling providence depend

---

[4] *Ibid.*; Bassett (ed.), *Correspondence*, II, 163.

the rise and prosperity, as well as the decline and downfall of empires." [5]

When Father Dubourg finished his address he presented Jackson with a wreath of laurel which he desired him to accept as "the prize of victory, and the symbol of immortality."

Jackson accepted the pledge and said: "Reverend Sir, I receive with gratitude and pleasure the symbolical crown which piety has prepared. I receive it in the name of the brave men who have so effectually seconded my exertions for the preservation of the country—they well deserve the laurels which their country will bestow." [6]

Then Jackson was escorted to a chair near the altar and Father Dubourg began the mass. While *Te Deum* was sung and the organ played music composed especially for the occasion, one of the mothers silently observed Jackson and later wrote: "I was seated in the very place I would have selected if my choice had been offered me of all the seats in the chapel—one person separated me from the dear old general, who sat on a chair rather apart, and I had a fine opportunity of contemplating his profile. I did not give the general one flower, but I could have given him many tears—one of the ladies reproved me laughingly for defrauding the general, whilst I stood unconsciously grasping the flowers which had been given me to strew." [7]

After the service was over, Jackson returned to his quarters to renew the defense of New Orleans and Louisiana. He sent reinforcements to the right bank of the river, and orders to keep a strict watch to his outposts on Bayou Lafourche and to Major Reynolds at The Temple. Some Kentucky troops and Louisiana Militia were stationed below the city while other Louisiana Militia guarded the Chef Menteur sector. The Tennesseans were sent to their previous camp on Avart plantation four miles above New Orleans. Baratarians and Mississippians prowled at large and kept Jackson informed of movements of the British. Because of the information they brought him, Jackson did not dare relax martial law.

---

[5] Latour, *Historical Memoir*, Appendix No. XXV, lxxi-lxxiii.

[6] *Ibid.;* Frost, *Pictorial Life of Andrew Jackson*, 399.

[7] Letter dated New Orleans, February 3, 1815, in *Niles' Register*, supplement to Vol. VIII, 163.

The British were on Lake Borgne. Lambert and Cochrane were planning to take Mobile in an attempt to reach the Mississippi overland from that direction. First, they would have to take Fort Bowyer. Jackson did not know of these plans but Baratarian scouts had informed him that on the 20th of January transports had arrived bringing two regiments of infantry from England. By March 10th, the total of reinforcements arriving on British transports was five regiments of infantry, three companies of garrison artillery, and a company of engineers—a total of 5,600 reinforcements.[8]

On February 8, the British made their first move against Fort Bowyer. Two and a half miles east of the fort, Lambert landed the second brigade, 1,200 strong, and 450 artillerists, sappers, miners, and marines. These established a line across the peninsula to cut off reinforcements from the mainland and at the same time they fortified sand mounds which the American gunners could not destroy.

Major Lawrence's garrison of 366 men had no protection against explosives thrown into the fort from the land side. At ten o'clock on the morning of February 11, Lambert sent a flag of truce with the demand that the fort surrender. Lawrence asked for time to consider and after consulting with his officers agreed to surrender the following day.

Meanwhile, Jackson had sent Livingston with a committee to the British fleet to negotiate for the exchange of prisoners and the return of nearly 200 slaves which had been taken away by the British army. Livingston and his committee arrived just as Lambert and Cochrane were preparing to take Fort Bowyer. They were received on the flagship and detained several days.

Two days after the surrender of Fort Bowyer, the British sloop *Brazen* arrived with news of peace. Then Livingston and his committee were permitted to return to New Orleans. They told Jackson about the peace. Jackson replied that the Treaty of Ghent had not been officially announced, that it was not valid until ratified by our government, and that they must not be thrown off guard. In other

---

[8] Buell, *History of Jackson*, II, 47-48.

words: Jackson could not disband his army while the enemy were in force on the coast, and martial law was still in effect.

Until this unofficial news of peace arrived, the civil authorities had not openly protested martial law and not too many militiamen had deserted their posts. But now Governor Claiborne appealed to Jackson to disband the army.

Jackson resented this interference and refused to comply, but the Creole volunteers and militia who lived in New Orleans wanted to return to their homes. As Marigny explained: " They wished to see their wives or mistresses; and they wanted to relate what they had done and what they had seen." [9]

These troops began to leave their stations with or without leave. A sharp reprimand from Jackson halted this method of escape but the Creoles thought of another. They went to Louis de Tousard, the French Consul, registered as French citizens and then applied to Jackson for discharge from military service. The first of these applications were granted but as the number increased Jackson's temper flared. He ordered all French citizens to retire into the interior, to a distance not nearer than Baton Rouge. Travel distance between New Orleans and Baton Rouge at this time was one hundred and twenty miles.

Tousard went to Governor Claiborne to get protection for French subjects. Jackson heard of this and ordered Tousard out of the city also. He went.

The French were indignant. Was this their reward for winning the Battle of New Orleans? Jackson could have done nothing without them—" he had been guided entirely by French officers in all his measures of defence. Were not the fortifications planned by Lafon, Latour and others? Was not Captain St. Gème of the dismounted dragoons, always at his elbow, and suggesting all his military movements? Had not Flaugeac, Beluche, Dominique and Laffite won the battle of the 8th of January with their artillery? " [10]

An anonymous letter appeared in *La Courrière de la Louisiane*

[9] Marigny, *Reflection on the Campaign*, 7.
[10] Gayarré, *History of Louisiana*, IV, 582.

which accused Jackson of abusing his authority when he ordered all Frenchmen residing in New Orleans to leave within three days and to keep at a distance of one hundred and twenty miles. As Jackson read the letter he fumed at what he considered defiance of military power. He ferreted out the author—Louaillier, the same who in December had defied him in the legislature—and had him arrested. Louaillier's counsel applied to Judge Hall for release on a writ of habeas corpus. Judge Hall granted the writ " to liberate the person of M. Louaillier."

Jackson grimly declared that this was a violation of his jurisdiction under martial law, so he had the judge arrested and conducted beyond the limits of the city with orders not to return until such time as peace was officially announced or the enemy had departed from the coast.

While this little squall was becoming a tempest, Gambie rounded up thirty Baratarians and walked off with two of Jackson's cannon— a 6-pounder and a 9-pounder. Perhaps Gambie felt he was only taking cannon which had been loaned for the defence of New Orleans. He got his men and cannon across the Mississippi to pirogues at the head of the bayous. There he learned that the mouths of the bayous were still obstructed by Jackson's orders. There was no point in trying to get to Grande Terre by way of Bayou Lafourche because it was very shallow at this time. The best route would be to get by Major Reynolds at The Temple and after that it would be easy to clear Degruy's Canal and reach the Gulf.

The main obstacle was Major Reynolds. He had strict orders to let no one pass without permission from General Jackson. Gambie knew this. He felt the pocket of his shirt. Yes, the paper was still there. His little fleet continued on to The Temple. When Major Reynolds stopped it, Gambie pulled the paper from his shirt and handed it to the major. It was a passport from General Jackson's headquarters giving Gambie permission to take men and two guns to Chernière Caminada for the defence of that place. The passport was signed by Edward Livingston, Jackson's chief aide.[11]

---

[11] USDC of La., Cases No. 817, No. 844.

Major Reynolds let the pirogues pass but he had his doubts when he saw Gambie and his men scramble to open Degruy's Canal. He immediately sent a report to General Jackson. Jackson's blood pressure went up. He stamped the floor in his rage (witnesses testified in court that he did so), but Jackson could do nothing. Official news of peace arrived and ended his military rule.

Judge Hall returned to the city. He waited until the rejoicings over peace had died down before he issued a writ summoning Jackson " to shew cause, on Friday next, the 24th March, at 10 o'clock A. M. inst., why an attachment should not be awarded against him, for contempts of this Court, in having disrespectfully wrested from the clerk aforesaid an original order of the Honorable the Judge of this Court, for the issuing of a writ of Habeas Corpus in the case of a certain Louaillier, then imprisoned by the said Major General Andrew Jackson, and for detaining the same, also for disregarding the said writ of Habeas Corpus when issued and served, in having imprisoned the Hon. the Judge of this Court, and for other contempts as stated by the witnesses." [12]

Jackson's aide-de-camp, John Reid, represented Old Hickory at the bar. He began to read a formal protest which said that contempt had not been committed in court, that the proceedings were illegal and unconstitutional, and that if Jackson were guilty of any statutory offence he had the right to trial by jury and not by a single judge. Only a few sentences of this defence had been read when the judge interrupted and ordered " the attachment to be sued out; " the process to be returnable on the 31st of March.

On that day an immense throng filled Royal Street in front of the little red-tiled court house. Dominique, Beluche, and about fifty Baratarians pushed their way into the crowded building. They didn't like Judge Hall. They had been hailed before him on too many occasions in this very court room. Jackson, dressed as a private citizen, had nearly reached the bar before Dominique spotted him.

" Général! " he yelled, " say the word and we pitch the judge and the bloody courthouse in the river! " [13]

---

[12] *Ibid.*, Case No. 791.   [13] Gayarré, *History of Louisiana*, IV, 620.

THE OLD COURT-HOUSE.

Pandemonium broke loose. Yells and shrieks rocked the room and the crowd outside wondered at the uproar. Jackson climbed on a bench and raised his hand. The tumult subsided and he spoke to the Baratarians of the respect due to public authorities and said that if they had any regard for him they would on this occasion forbear expressing their feelings and opinions.

In the silence that followed Judge Hall directed the clerk to proceed. He called the case: " The United States versus Andrew Jackson."

Then the District Attorney presented nineteen interrogatories to Jackson saying: " Did you not arrest Louaillier? Did you not arrest the judge of this court? Did you not seize the writ of habeas corpus? Did you not say a variety of disrespectful things to the judge? "

Jackson informed the court that he would not be interrogated. He said: " You would not hear my defence. . . . Under these circumstances, I appear before you, to receive the sentence of the court, and have nothing further to add." [14]

---

[14] Reid and Eaton, *Life of Jackson*, 387.

Since Jackson did not answer the interrogatories the court had no alternative but to adjudge him in contempt. As Judge Hall pronounced the sentence—a fine of $1,000—he said that the duty was unpleasant, that he could not forget the important services of the the defendant to his country, and that in consideration thereof he would not make imprisonment a part of the punishment. " The only question," he added, " is whether the Law should bend to the General or the General to the Law." [15]

Jackson bowed to the judge and started to walk away, but Dominique and Beluche and others lifted him on their shoulders and bore him triumphantly from the room. They placed him in a carriage from which the horses had been unhitched and " amidst the huzzas of an immense concurse " Jackson was taken by his admirers to the Exchange Coffee House.

There he spoke to them saying: " During the invasion I exerted every one of my faculties for the defence and preservation of the Constitution and the laws. On this day, I have been called on to submit to their operation under circumstances which many persons might have thought sufficient to justify resistance. Considering obedience to the laws, even when we think them unjustly applied, as the first duty of the citizen, I did not hesitate to comply with the sentence you have heard pronounced, and I entreat you to remember the example I have given you of respectful submission to the administration of Justice." [16]

---

[15] Bassett, *Life of Jackson*, 229.
[16] Gayarré, *History of Louisiana*, IV, 625.

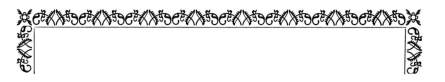

TAPS

GENERAL JACKSON AND THE LEGISLATURE OF LOUISIANA EARN-
estly recommended to the President of the United States that the
Baratarians be given a full pardon. Not only did James Madison
grant this pardon; but he also authorized that all suits, indictments and prosecutions against them " be stayed, discontinued and
released."

However, it was difficult for most of the Baratarians to settle
down to the humdrum of legitimate business. Gambie never did.
His ship the *Philanthrope*, which Patterson had taken as prize to
New Orleans when he destroyed the establishment on Grande Terre,
had been sold to Julius Caesar Amigoni and renamed *Le Petit Milan*.
Amigoni was just a front. The real owners were New Orleans
merchants and lawyers who belonged to the Mexican Association.
They wanted Mexico to become independent of Spain so that they
could trade with that country and be paid in hard money, still a
very scarce item in the United States.[1]

Many Mexican patriots had been in New Orleans throughout the
battle and their leader, General José Alvarez de Toledo, was able
to persuade Jackson that important dispatches must be sent to

---

[1] This paragraph and the following are based on testimony found in USDC of La.,
Cases No. 817, No. 821, No. 824, No. 844.

patriots in Mexico. Early in February Jackson granted permission for *Le Petit Milan* to sail with these dispatches on condition that she go without arms and commit no depredations on Spanish commerce. Toledo agreed to this *in writing.* Then *Le Petit Milan* dropped innocently down river with Julius Caesar Amigoni in command. The vessel went out Southwest Pass and headed for Grande Isle.

Gambie was there with his two cannon. He mounted them on the vessel, took on board twenty men from Grande Isle and the ones he had brought with him, changed the name of the ship to *L'Aigle*, and sailed against Spanish shipping under a Mexican privateer commission. Along the coast between Tampico and Vera Cruz he captured a vessel with a cargo of flour, beef, tallow, sheep, and a bag containing $1,000.

Gambie landed on the coast and sold the ship and its cargo to Mexican patriots. He kept the $1,000 and the clothing of the crew. Two days later at seven o'clock in the morning, he made another prize, *La Santa Rita.* She was laden with brandy, wine, and dry goods. Gambie transferred her crew to the hold of *L'Aigle* and put a prize crew on board *La Santa Rita.*

At seven that night he captured another vessel, *El Presidente,* with a cargo of dry goods, oil in jars, iron, and white wine in barrels.

Gambie sailed east with his two prizes. He passed Isle Dernière and came to Cat Island where he anchored when he saw a number of small craft there. Within three days he was able to unload his loot and get it smuggled up Bayou Lafourche and across to New Orleans. Then United States gunboats appeared and took possession of Gambie's three schooners. Gambie asked permission to go on shore and get oysters for his crew. He did not return. This happened in the month of April.

Early in May the United States Marshal was ordered to bring Vincent Gambie into the Federal District Court because he did " illegally fit out and arm or was knowingly concerned in the fitting out and arming of a certain schooner called *The Eagle,* alias *Petit Milan,* alias *Philanthrope,* with intent that said schooner should be employed in the service of some foreign prince or state to cruise or commit hostilities upon the subjects, citizens or property of another foreign prince or state, with whom the United States are at peace."

On May 6, a Federal Grand Jury indicted Gambie for piracy. Étienne de Boré, the famous Étienne de Boré who had made Louisiana sugar granulate, went Gambie's bail for the sum of $8,000. But then, De Boré had nothing to fear because, as Vincent Nolte said, no man in the United States knew better than Edward Livingston how to draw up a bond so that the sum mentioned never could be demanded by law from the bailer.[2]

Gambie was tried in the red-tiled court house on Royal Street. The verdict was, " Not guilty."

For the next few years, Gambie sailed on his own and there is no record of his piracy other than hearsay. Then one day he was sailing north of Haiti when he spotted a sail. As it came closer he recognized Jean Laffite. Gambie's smouldering revenge burst into flame and he ordered his crew to fire on Jean Laffite. Jean's guns answered and the battle raged till dark. Both captains made repairs during the night and at the crack of dawn Gambie attacked again. Within two hours the battle was over and Laffite watched Gambie and his ship sink beneath the waves.

After the Battle of New Orleans, Beluche and perhaps two hundred Baratarians raided Spanish shipping under letters of marque from Cartagena. There is no way of knowing how many prizes they made during 1815. The only ones for which there are records are those which were libelled in federal court.

Two of Beluche's vessels, *La Popa* and the *Piñeres*, sailed through the Spanish blockade and into Cartagena Bay in August, 1815. They were laden with provisions for starving patriots. Soon the Spanish army had possession of all land approaches to the city while forty of their vessels blockaded Cartagena by sea. The patriots asked

---

[2] *Fifty Years in Both Hemispheres*, 230.

Beluche to take a letter to Simón Bolívar who was then in Jamaica. Beluche, in *La Popa*, thumbed his nose at the Spanish, got through the blockade and delivered the letter to the Liberator.

Bolívar and Beluche decided to go first to Les Cayes in Haiti where they hoped to find supplies and ammunition before sailing for Cartagena.[3] Soon after they arrived at Les Cayes four hundred refugees reached there and told them of the fall of Cartagena. While Bolívar organized them for an invasion of South America, Beluche outfitted the ships—rounding up crewmen and supplies in his usual manner. Prowling to the west of Haiti, he spied the *Santa Rosa*. She had taken on a merchant cargo at Jamaica and had left the port of Kingston on January 5, 1816. Beluche captured her the next day. He put the crew in chains but let the captain and supercargoes go free. Sailing back to Haiti, Beluche signalled outside the harbor of Les Cayes to one of the privateers who joined him and then the three vessels sailed to the bay of Haquen.

There, marks on the boxes and bales were erased and new ones put in their places. While this was being done, the value of the cargo was estimated to be $40,000. It was landed and sold for $30,000 to a Frenchman who speculated in such merchandise. Soon Beluche took another prize. Then an American schooner hailed him and the captain informed Beluche that a Spanish warship from Cartagena was after him. This made Beluche laugh and say, " I would like to meet that warship." [4]

Beluche returned to Les Cayes and found that his *Piñeres* had arrived. President Petion gave orders to the Governor of Les Cayes to let Bolívar have powder, lead, muskets, and a printing press. In addition, he ordered three Haitian transports to accompany Bolívar's expedition. These with two Cartagenan schooners and

---

[3] Alfredo Boulton, *Miranda, Bolívar y Sucre* (Caracas, 1959), 48-55.

[4] When the captain of the captured *Santa Rosa* reached Cuba, he reported that Beluche's *La Popa* had a crew of 100 and was armed with one 16-pound cannon, one 12-pound swivel, 12 small bronze cannon, and 50 muskets. The captain referred to Beluche as " Mr. Pierry." This was one of several aliases used by Beluche. Corráles, *Documentos para la historia de Cartagena*, II, 295-300.

Beluche's two made a grand total of seven little vessels which left Les Cayes at the end of March, 1816, " to begin the conquest of half a continent."

La Popa now had a new name, the *General Bolívar*, and being the best armed and the fastest, became the flagship. Bolívar and most of his officers sailed on the flagship—and so Beluche started on his fabulous career as the most famous admiral in Bolívar's navy. But that story will fill another volume.

After South America's wars for independence were over, Beluche became a Venezuelan citizen and to the end of his long life was always involved in turbulent episodes. He died and was buried in Puerto Cabello. The slab over his grave bears this inscription:

General Renato Beluche
Octubre 4, 1860
79 años [5]

Chighizola and other Baratarians returned to the peaceful life of oyster fishing and sailing shrimp boats. Chighizola became the patriarch of Grande Isle and his descendants there today will show visitors with pride the tomb that covers his remains.

For several years Jean and Pierre Laffite held together a privateer establishment at Galveston, but this was abandoned in 1821. Later Jean changed his name to John Lafflin and dropped out of sight. He must have laughed many times to himself as the Laffite legend grew. His brother Pierre died in 1844 in the small Missouri town of Crèvecoeur and was buried in the Wesleyan Cemetery of St. Louis.

Jean's son wrote in the family Bible on May 5, 1854, at Alton, Illinois:

---

[5] When Beluche received top ranking in the navy, he was given the title of general and not admiral because he was expected to fight on land as well as on sea; and perhaps also because of the sorry career of the only officer who had been given the title of admiral—Luis Brion.

Our father died. Will be with
our brother Glenn Henri: Will be
with Uncle Pierre in Heaven.[6]

And what about the little man who had been born in Haiti and christened Alexandre Frederic Laffite but who, as Dominique You, had carried Andrew Jackson on his shoulders?

Dominique could not forget the words of praise bestowed on him when Jackson reviewed the troops and said: "Captains Dominique and Belluche . . . were stationed at Nos. 3 and 4. The general cannot avoid giving his warm approbation . . . of the gallantry with which they have redeemed the pledge they gave at the opening of the campaign to defend the country."

Dominique *was* an American patriot. He sailed a few times for his brothers and then returned to New Orleans where he acquired a tavern at the end of St. Anne Street.

For a few years Dominique was happy. Then head injuries he had received in the past and evil effects of the months spent in a damp Cabildo cell began to take their toll. Headaches and body pains became more frequent. The last ten years of his life were a slow, torturous death. His tavern became neglected, squalid.

Dominique You died on November 14, 1830.

Flags were lowered to half-mast and all business houses closed. That afternoon *L'Abeille* and other newspapers published notices calling on all friends of Dominique to attend his funeral. Under large headlines cannoneers of the Battalion of Artillery and the Louisiana Legion were notified to assist at the funeral next day.

Dominique's earthly remains were taken to the Cathedral for the rites of the Catholic Church. Then a military escort and a great throng of people accompanied them to St. Louis Cemetery No. 2 where he was interred with full military honors.

When the last gun had been fired, a little group of men gathered around the tomb as Masons are wont to do.[7] One of them stepped forward to deliver the oration.

---

[6] Arthur, *Jean Laffite*, 238-53, 256, 279.
[7] Dominique was a member of lodge La Concorde No. 3. Arthur, *Jean Laffite*, 234.

" My friends," he said, " the worthy citizen, the brave warrior, the intrepid seaman, captain Dominique You, ceased to exist yesterday. . . . The authorities wishing to render funeral honors which were due to his remains, caused his corpse to be carried to the Cathedral Church; and thence you have seen him transported to his last abode, attended by the officers of the military and soldiers under arms, carrying their flag. . . . There only remains for us to repeat the words pronounced on his tomb by the worthy pastor Moni: *Requiescat in pace*; Rest in peace. . . . This is the solemn wish of Louisianians in memory of the services rendered by captain Dominique, in the engagements of the 23rd of December, 1814, and 8th of January, 1815, the time of the defeat of the English." [8]

When the oration was finished, each man in the circle slowly filed by the tomb, dropped a sprig of evergreen, and said: "Alas! My brother! "

---

[8] *Ibid.*, 234-35.

APPENDIX A

Donaldson Ville Feb. 18th 1814

Dear Sir:

I rec^d your letter of the 4th instant by Mr Gilmore yesterday—Nothing could give me more pleasure than to here of your intention to communicate to our Government a statement of this banditti, the most base and daring ever known in any country on Earth—this outlawd crew of which you have requested information are established on an Island known by the name of Cat Island situated about fifteen miles to the west of the mouth of the La Fourche, their force consists of five or six armed vessels, carrying from 12, to 14, guns each and from 60 to 90. men—They have some heavy cannon on the Island and also a gun Brig sunk in the pass on which they have a battery of 14. guns.— From the best information I can obtain their crews when collected amount to from 5. to 600, men, and I have not a doubt but the advantage of their position triple their force against an offensive operation which could be carried on only in Barges, for the numerous shoals form a barrier against vessels of any considerable size without a correct chart—The quantity of goods brought in by this banditti is immense: I have not a doubt but they have entered & secured for more than a million of dollars within this last six months.—When once their goods are deposited in New Orleans they apprehend no danger of being detected, for they even offer them at public auction, and they have but few difficulties in getting them transported there, for nine tenth of the community are proud to support and protect this infernal crew:— I am informed, that as many as 500, hundred [sic.] inhabitants, & citizens of New Orleans have been seen at one time on this Island to purchase and brig away goods—What depravity!—Men in office; Citizens hitherto of undoubted integrity and first respectability, uniting with a piratical band and sharing with them their ill gotten booty—When officers no longer regard their oaths citizens may (with) impunity lay aside their integrity and the opposition to law and justice consequently become meratorious:— Such, I conceive to be our present situation, and him who, once placed unbounded confidence in the loyalty of his subjects has this day proofs sufficiently demonstrative of his error, and in my opinion if things do not change, will ere long be obliged to claim protection of the General Government for his own personal safety This will not be credited, but a fact well known, that a reward of five hundred dollars having been offered by the Gov. to any person that would apprehend Le Fitte was sneered at as being contemptable and in reply 5000. $. was offered by Le Fitte & Party, for the apprehension and safely conveying to the Isle *au Chat* his Excellency—and I firmly believe that the Gov. runs a greater risk of being taken to Cat Island and tried for his life than Le Fitte does of being punished for his crimes in the State of Louisiana— It is a fact they have at this time several men attached to the custom house in close confinement and a custom house officer sentenced to ten years hard Labor with a 56. pound weight hung to his leg—their unherd of depredations will not be believed but they are facts and some of the most enormous I have been an eye witness—

I am Sir,

With the highest esteem & respect

your obed^t Servt

Walker Gilbert

Thos. Freeman Esquire

Records of the Eastern District, State Land Office of Louisiana

APPENDIX B

The original copy of the Roster of the Orleans Battalion is contained in the Louisiana State Department of Archives, Baton Rouge, Louisiana.

Translation of title:

Staff of the Troops of the Orleans Battalion under the orders of Major J. B. Plauché on December 20, 1814.

Etat Major de la Force du
Bataillon d'Orleans sous les ordres
du Major J. B. Plauché le
20 Decembre 1814.

Etat Major

J. B. Plauché   Major   C. Sainet   Quartier Mai.
F. M. Reynaud   adjt.   J. Le Monnier   Chirurgi.
Casper Joy   "

Compagnie
des Carabiniers

		Soldats.
Pierre Roche	Capt.	B. Génois
Coeur de Roy	1er Lieut	Obignon
B. Grima	2. "	Chaumette
L. Roche	3 "	J. Bozant
A. Tourla	1er Sergt.	D'aphremont
Soubercaze	2 "	B. Bozant
J. Desvignes	3 "	Millaudon
Guadz	4 "	Jean Bart
Turtin aîné	5 "	Papet
A. Choppin	6 "	Picena
Lanaux	7 "	Michel Armat
S. Alvarez	Fournier	Tricou
A. Liautand	1er Caporal	Chastant
Marchand	2 "	Bacas
Tremoulet	3 "	Labarre
Bel aîné	4 "	Garcia
Guesnard	5 "	Cohn.
G. S. Forstall	6 "	Vanel.
Isnard	7 "	Lucas
Rondeau	8 "	

A. Lemoine   J. B. Voisin
Durel aîné   Sagory

Musiciens

Pommier	Foucher
Maurice	Valentine
Cahony	Trimé
J. B. Fagot	Dufilho
Cruzel	Carry
A. Fernandez	Cronin
Tessier	Puech Jr.
Desforges	S. Fauchet
Denis	Lacroix

Compagnie des Dragons
(a pied)

Huy. St Geme	Capt	Defourge
J. St Jean	1er Lieut	C. Bélot
Benetaud	2 "	C. Lemaître
Dulcot	3 "	S. Cohn
Huet	4 "	Enard
A. Bonneval	M. Logis chef	Hanbert
J. B. Joublanc	" "	Brelet
J. B. Lattens		Durand fils
Gautier	1er Brigadier	David
Mioton	2 "	Porte aîné
Dubignon	3 "	Ferrand
J. B. Hacker	4 "	

Pajand	St Armand.
Syler	Garridel
Ducayet	La Borde
Ferrera	Morel.
Orteing	S. Paxton
Turpin Jr.	H McCall
F. Sibilot	C. F. Vizinier
Pellerin	F. Duplessis
St Cyr	Foucher
Desforges	Berluchaux
N. Durel.	Golis
Devize	Porche fils
Jourdain	Seignouret
Morze.	Morin
V. Jourdain	Détour
Delarue	Tete
J. Hart	Avart
Trépagnier	J. R. Stringer
Desmarates	Coignard.
Pidesclaux	F. Funel.
P Pidesclaux	Fagot
P Lanaux	Liberal
J. H. Shepherd	Bufac
Barthelmy	A. Gervais
P De Buys	P. Wale
W De Buys	H. Mercier
M. Sarge	St Avid.
Barbarin.	V. Nolté
G. Musson.	Roland
Moro	Tremoulet
S Marchand	A. Prieur
Drouet	V. Lessassier

Compagnie des Chasseurs

A. Guibert, Capt.

J. C. de St. Comes	1st Lieut.	Lamothe fils	5 Sergt
Louis Pilie	2 "	St. Cyr	6 "
Gueronard	1 Sergt.	Cavaillee	Fourrier "
Couvertie aine	2 "	Fradaud	1 Capl.
Couvertie jeune	3 "	Pesson	2 "
Pidoux	4 "	Ducayet	3 "
		Bouny	4 "

Soldats

Schomberg	J. Montamat
Mahé	Lavan
J. B. Lefretre	Gourson
Lesconflair	Gilly
Macoin	Barbarin
Mariot	Michault
Dufry	N. Parisien
Chazal	Cheminard
B. Blaumé	Ricaud
Mc. Clelland	C. Lefevre
Baptiste	A. Gravier
Dufuy	A. Richard
Daunoy	J. B. Blanchard
M. Meilleur	Maison Rouge
S. M. Lafrice	Fort
Galliot	Verron
Lemoine père	J. Berluchaux
Bournos	J. Bonabel
Delamothe	Jice
Maurian	V. Lefevre
Carraby	Lafferandrie

(166)

Rivaux	Riviere
Clairvaux	Badigée
Bicombelle	Jerome
Lebros	Badin

Compagnie des Francs

J. Kudry	Capt	A. Robert	4 Sergt
S. Fremont	1.r Lieut	Bible	1. Fourrier 5 ,,
E. Bertel	2 ,,	E. Touchet	1. Capor.
Chevalon	Sergt Major	E. Sperrier	2 ,,
Jerome Tourné	2 Sergt	N. Vassel	3 ,,
Giraudau	3 ,,	J. Guerin	4 ,,

Soldats

Bayard	J. Sifflet
N. Molé	Cuivillier
F. Thercout	Bonnaventure
T. Hoffman	L. Ayot
M. Thomas	Sanschagrun
G. Rolland	Charles Fé
J. Lemaitre	Desbans
Niniche	P. Landreaux
P. Sitet	Grégoire
B. Rolland	T. Duricon
T. Ribard	Bolence
Hyp Dubensir	T. D. Henry
L. Hugot	J. Freinden
C. Mayer	J. Toledano
C. Toledano	A. Grimden
A. Toledano	T. Hoffman
B. Frederic	J. Muller

Dragons

Saulet	Lambert
M. Destouche	Bise
Despris	B. Desonges
Marans	Simillien
Marin	Le Bon
Pons	La Barrière
Mercier	Pode
N. Frederic	Menard
Bouillet	Barnett
Cadion	S. Marat
Ducoin	Camas
Michel	Duheron
Theon	Noisé
Raymond	Marcenat
Jériet	Calabour
Cruzel	Raymond
Durand	Corobolles ainé
Michel Gautier	Corobolles cadet
Rouchet	Cérisol
Guignan	Juette
Arbt	Barthelemy
B. Andigé	Piquerin
Le Beau	Murol
Chassagne	Duplantier
J. Perier	Ramel
Charleville	Lauzun
Pellier	A. Larin
Danse	J. B. Tripot
Leloup	St Jean
Mouton	L. Nicolas

Joe. Bourgeois   A. Guillemin

St Germain   L. Lafitte

Grosset.

Compagnie de Louisiana Blues

Mansel White   Capitaine

J.S. Girault	1st Lieut	Garlick	3. Sergt.
N. Thompson	2 "	W.J. Gorham	Fourrier
J. Philips	1 Sergt	Scott	1. Caporal
R. Nisbett	2 "	Goforth	2 "

Soldats

McFarland	J. Hull
Durive	J. Major
Packwood	Hubbard
Deruse	T. Laidlaw
Cotton	Cornico
Millon	J. C. Nichols
J. Hagan	Bronden
Jones	Armstrong
C. Dameron	J. Belize
J. Prior	John Scharp
Hays	Moore
J. Nuggat	J. McClelland
H. W. Palfrey	Lee White.
J. Nednur	W McClelland.
Smith	Jourdan
D. P. Ruff	R. Dobbs
J. Lambert	C. Beans
	Nichols

J. B. Sel.
C. Vallé
Brouet
Gervais
Rolland.
Sibilot
T. Veau
A. Peuroux
Castinet
Ch.ᵗ Duchamp
Dufouchard.

Guerin
Bourque
Moun
Lambert
B. Duchamp
Sibilot aîné
Hachard
Mennier
S. Hiriart
Bournos aîné
De Gruy

ESSAY ON AUTHORITIES

The richest primary sources for information on the Baratarians are: Archives of the United States District Court of Louisiana District in New Orleans; United States Customs Archives for the port of New Orleans; National Archives, Washington, D. C., *Sección Venezolana del Archivo de la Gran Colombia*, Caracas; *Archivo Nacional*, Bogotá; *Archivo General de Indias*, Seville (typescripts, Edward E. Ayer Collection, Newberry Library, Chicago); Saint Louis Cathedral Archives, New Orleans; Cabildo Records, New Orleans; Howard Tilton Memorial Library Archives, New Orleans; Louisiana State University Archives, Baton Rouge; *Journal of Jean Laffite* (New York, 1958); and Laffite papers in the *Bibliotheca Parsoniana* which was in New Orleans at the time this study was made.

The United States District Court of Louisiana District was established in New Orleans in 1806. In its archives are Case Papers, Minute Books, and other documents pertaining to trials and indictments. Lyle Saxon's *Laffite the Pirate* has fascinated readers since it was first published in New York in 1930; however, it is a loss both to scholarship and literature that Saxon did not use the mass of federal court records in New Orleans. His devotees say they were not available. Under the Work Projects Administration, Louisiana State University sponsored a survey of federal archives in the state. Stanley Clisby Arthur, state supervisor of this project, directed the preparation of an indexed typescript of *Conspicuous Cases in the United States District Court of Louisiana*. Five copies were made in 1940, and one set is in the Louisiana State University Archives. Arthur's *Jean Laffite, Gentleman Rover* (New Orleans, 1952), has great merit since it is based on court records and on some of the Jean Laffite papers in the possession of John A. Laffite.

The Laffite correspondence concerning British intrigue was filed with Case

Papers in the USDC of La. These were acquired by E. A. Parsons and in his article " Jean Laffite in the War of 1812," in *Proceedings of the American Antiquarian Society*, L, Part 2 (Worcester, October 16, 1940), he gives their exact location in *Bibliotheca Parsoniana*.

United States Customs Archives for the Port of New Orleans contain " Crew Lists," " Ship Registers and Enrollments," and " Returns of Seamen for Marine Hospital Tax." From time to time customs records have been sent to the National Archives, Washington, D. C. After examination there, some have been kept and the rest returned to New Orleans.

From late 1811 until the fall of Cartagena to the Spanish in December, 1815, Baratarians sailed under letters of marque from that place. Not only did they destroy Spanish shipping, but many served in the Cartagenan navy. Outstanding among these was Renato Beluche, a native of New Orleans, who after the fall of Cartagena outfitted a fleet for Simón Bolívar which sailed for South America in 1816. The expedition succeeded in making the island of Margarita a base from which Bolívar or his officers could issue privateer commissions. Not only Beluche but other Baratarians sailed under these licenses for the next eight or nine years. Nearly all the original records that have survived are in the *Archivo Nacional* at Bogotá. Included are hundreds of letters to and from Beluche and service records for him and other privateers who helped South America win its independence from Spain.

The author has examined other archives in Haiti, Caracas, Lima, Guayaquil, Quito, and Panama, only to find that Bolívar and his secretaries had sent most of the records to Bogotá. Three times the author went to Bogotá to investigate the tons of records there, and each time felt helpless and frustrated. She could only skim the small part which had been catalogued or bound in large volumes which contain a thousand or more items.

The *Fundación John Boulton* was organized in Caracas in 1950 by H. L. Boulton y Co., S. A. It has completed microfilming all items in the Bogotá archives that have any bearing on Venezuelan history. This is now the *Sección Venezolana del Archivo de la Gran Colombia* and contains more than 210,000 photographs. These are being placed on microcards, analyzed and catalogued. When they have been processed, the microcards will be available to any researcher.

This author has only a few photostats of documents in the *Archivo General de Indias*. She has relied on the pioneer research of Stanley Faye in the sections that concern privateers. Faye published the following articles in the *Louisiana Historical Quarterly*, Baton Rouge: " Privateersmen of the Gulf and Their Prizes," XXII, No. 4 (October, 1939) ; " Privateers of Guadeloupe and Their Establishment in Barataria," XXIII, No. 2 (April, 1940) ; " The

Great Stroke of Pierre Laffite," XXIII, No. 3 (July, 1940); and " Commodore Aury," XXIV, No. 3 (July, 1941).

Between 1845 and 1850, Jean Laffite wrote a diary in French. He requested his heirs not to let it be published for 107 years. His direct descendant, John A. Laffite, published an unedited, English translation in New York in 1958. That part of *The Journal of Jean Laffite* which deals with the years 1804 to about 1825 is an amazing complement to Case Papers in USDC of La. and to material in the other archives mentioned above. This *Journal* needs to be edited by a historian thoroughly familiar with the period 1800 to 1850.

The last three volumes of Henry Adams, *History of the United States of America* (9 vols., New York, 1890 and 1930), deals with the United States during the administration of James Madison. These volumes are still the best history of the War of 1812. A. T. Mahan, *Sea Power in its Relation to the War of 1812* (2 vols., Boston, 1905), rates second. English historians have more or less ignored this war. One exception is the mediocre work of William James, *A Full and Correct Account of the Military Occurrences of the Late War Between Great Britain and the United States of America* (2 vols., London, 1818). More recently, Winston S. Churchill, *The Age of Revolution* (New York, 1957, vol. 3 of *A History of the English-Speaking Peoples*), deals with the war in a brief ten-page chapter which charges that the War Hawks were responsible for causing it because they wanted Canada and had no conception of affairs in Europe. C. S. Forester, *The Age of Fighting Sail* (New York, 1956), reads well.

For the invasion of Louisiana as reported by the defenders, Major A. Lacarrière Latour, *Historical Memoir of the War in West Florida and Louisiana in 1814-15*, with an *Atlas* (Philadelphia, 1816), heads the list. Vincent Nolte, *Fifty Years in Both Hemispheres* (New York, 1854), describes the episode as a business man saw it. The edited correspondence of two principal figures in the Battle of New Orleans gives an insight into the character and achievement of each. John Spencer Bassett (ed.), *Correspondence of Andrew Jackson* (7 vols., Washington, 1926-1935); and Dunbar Rowland (ed.), *Official Letter Books of W. C. C. Claiborne, 1801-1816* (6 vols., Jackson, 1907), have been frequently cited.

The reports that Jackson's aides and the naval officers sent to Washington and to newspapers must be taken with a grain of salt. These men gave themselves credit for victory over the British. Only rarely did they mention Baratarians or Creoles. They failed, for example, to file a single memorandum on such an important item as how many cannon, cannon balls, muskets, and flint, and how much cannister, round-shot, grape, bullets, and powder Laffite and his Baratarians supplied. Without these the outcome would have been different. Creoles and Baratarians were justly incensed as the legend grew that

Kentucky and Tennessee rifles had won the Battle of New Orleans. Bernard de Marigny, in his *Reflection on the Campaign of General Andrew Jackson in Louisiana 1814 and 1815*, typescript translation, WPA (New Orleans, 1939)—orignally published in French by J. L. Sollée (New Orleans, 1848)—was one of the few who cried out in print against this misrepresentation.

More reliable than official reports are the letters written in camp below New Orleans or in that city and sent to relatives and friends in eastern cities. Many of these were given to newspapers and periodicals. The most complete coverage of the defence of New Orleans with regard to these letters and to official reports as well, is to be found in *Niles' Register*, Vols. VI, VII, VIII (Balitmore, 1814-1815); and the 1815 issues of the Boston *Daily Advertiser and Repertory.*

For the British point of view on the invasion of Louisiana, one has to depend on memoirs of English officers who took part in the Chesapeake and Louisiana campaigns. The ones this author was able to locate are: Frederick Chamier, *The Life of a Sailor* (2 vols., New York, 1833); George Laval Chesterton, *Peace, War and Adventure* (2 vols., London, 1853); John Henry Cooke, *A Narrative of Events in the South of France and of the Attack on New Orleans, in 1814 and 1815* (London, 1835); Benson Earle Hill, *Recollections of an Artillery Officer* (2 vols., London, 1836); and a work of which there have been many editions, but of which this author has been able to collate only six: G. R. Gleig, *The Campaigns of the British Army at Washington and New Orleans, under Generals Ross, Pakenham, and Lambert, in the Years 1814-15* (London, 1821, 1826, 1833, and 1836)—published also without the author's name under the title *A Subaltern in America; Comprising His Narrative of the Campaigns of the British Army, at Baltimore, Washington, & &, During the Late War* (Philadelphia 1826 and 1833). The later editions have significant omissions and changes.

Many biographies of Jackson have appeared since the Battle of New Orleans, but only a few need be mentioned. Two works written by men who were close to the event and who knew the main characters were Alexander Walker, *Jackson and New Orleans* (New York, 1856); and James Parton, *Life of Andrew Jackson* (3 vols., New York, 1861). A third outstanding biography was published a half century later—Augustus C. Buell, *History of Andrew Jackson* (2 vols., New York, 1904). Then came John Spencer Bassett, *The Life of Andrew Jackson* (New York, 1925); and finally Marquis James, *Andrew Jackson, The Border Captain* (Indianapolis, 1933).

The illustrations are taken from Benson J. Lossing, *The Pictorial Field-Book of the War of 1812* (New York, 1869).

INDEX

lack of guns, 119; munitions supply, 122; food supply, 124; observes British from Macarty House, 127; sends Kentucky Militia to west bank, 129; river redoubt of, 131–32; troops of, on January 8, 132; surveys line, January 8, 132; praises Dominique, 133; outposts of, 134; in battle of January 8, 136–38; truce line of, 139; casualties of January 8, 139; surveys British camp, 141; General Orders of, January 21, 142–43; return of, to city, 143; triumph of, 144–46; sends Livingston to British fleet, 147; accused in *La Courrière*, 148–49; arrests Judge Hall, 149; ends martial law, 150; writ summoning, 150; contempt of court, 150–52; fined, 152; allows departure of *Le Petit Milan*, 153–54

Jones, Thomas Ap Catesby, 62, 65

Jugeat, Captain Pierre, 55, 84, 86, 87, 89, 130, 132, 143; organizes Choctaws, 78; on December 28, 106–107, terrorizes British, 112

Keane, Major General John, 30, 97; commands British Army, 67; reviews troops, 70; questions Joe Ducros, 73; decides to halt, 74; handbill of, 75; report of, on night battle, 94–95; receives reinforcements, 96; on December 28, 105; column of, along river, 130, 137; wounded, 137

Kemper, Reuben, reconnoiters, 125–26

Kentucky Militia, xi, 79, 83, 120, 146; on west bank, 129, 138; on Jackson's line, 132; Jackson's praise of, 143

Lacoste, Major Pierre, plantation of, 77, 88, 127; on Gentilly plain, 84; night battle on plantation of, 91; battalion of, 132

Laffite, Alexandre, 4, 5; *see* You, Dominique

Laffite, Denise Jeannette, 7n.

Laffite, Françoise Sel, 7n.

Laffite, Jean, 4, 5, 11, 17, 19, 35, 43, 52, 148, 155; Spanish spy, xii; description

of, 7; warehouses of, 13; auction of, at The Temple, 16; debt of, to United States, 20; writ for, 20; handbill of, 21, 161; magazines of, 23, 82; clash with Gambie, 24; well informed, 36; British approach, 37; bribe offered to, 40; answers British, 41; letter to Jean Blanque, 42; letter to Claiborne, 45–56; refuses British offer, 53; with Jackson, 81, 87; at The Temple, 82; advice of, on defense line, 101; installs 24's, 104; alias John Laffin, 157; death of, 157

Laffite, Maria Zora Nadrimal, 4

Laffite, Pierre, 4, 11, 16, 19; Spanish spy, xii; description of, 8; writ for, 20; in jail, 39–40, 43; escapes from jail, 44; reward for, 44; with Jackson, 87, 88; guides Coffee, 88; death of, 157

Lafourche, Bayou, 13, 46, 53, 146, 149, 154

Lakes
Borgne, 62, 63, 64, 68, 113, 147
Ouatchas, Big Lake of, 3; Little Lake of, 3, 16
Pontchartrain, 58, 62, 64, 82
Salvador, 3

Lambert, Major General John, arrival of, with two regiments, 123, 127; with reserves in rear, 130; commander in chief, 137–38; sends truce flag, 139; engineers of, build road, 140; retreat of, 140–41; at Mobile, 147

Laporte, Rosa, 6n.

Latour, Major Arsène Lacarrière, Spanish spy, xii; book of, xii, 3; reconnoiters, 84, 85, 86; description of, 85; estimates Jackson's forces, 87; on advantage of cannonading, 121; west bank defense of, 127–28; planned fortifications, 148

Lawrence, Major William, defense of Fort Bowyer, 51–53; remains at Fort Bowyer, 57; surrenders Fort Bowyer, 147

Levine, Christina, 6n.

Levine, Thomas, 6n.

Livingston, Edward, 20, 149; attorney

04-0